GOD *is in the* HOUSE

GOD *is in the* HOUSE

CONGRESSIONAL TESTIMONIES **OF FAITH**

VIRGINIA FOXX
MEMBER OF CONGRESS

Chapter quote pages, flag image: Shutterstock © STILLFX; background texture: Shutterstock © ilolab. Photographs of J. Randy Forbes and Dan Lipinski courtesy of their respective offices. All other photographs are from U.S. Government Publishing Office (gpo.gov). Public domain.

Visit us at ShadowMountain.com

Library of Congress Cataloging-in-Publication Data

Name: Foxx, Virginia, 1943– compiler.
Title: God is in the House : congressional testimonies of faith / compiled by Virginia Foxx, Ed.D., member of Congress
Description: Salt Lake City, Utah : Ensign Peak, [2016] | ?2016 | Includes bibliographical references.
Identifiers: LCCN 2016003790 (print) | LCCN 2016012420 (ebook) | ISBN 9781629722375 (paperbound : alk. paper) | ISBN 9781629734545 (ebook)
Subjects: LCSH: Legislators—Religious life—United States. | Legislators—United States—Biography. | United States. Congress. House—Biography. | Faith.
Classification: LCC JK1319 .G636 2016 (print) | LCC JK1319 (ebook) | DDC 270.092/273—dc23
LC record available at http://lccn.loc.gov/2016003790

Printed in the United States of America
Edwards Brothers Malloy, Ann Arbor, MI

10 9 8 7 6 5 4 3 2 1

CONTENTS

FOREWORD

These comments were originally delivered at a Catholic Prayer Breakfast in May 2016. But since the message is universal, I felt that it might also be of value to readers of this book.

Thomas Aquinas once wrote, "It should be known that all right-thinking men" (clearly, he never ran for office) "make contemplation of God the end of human life."

In other words, the purpose of human life—*our* purpose—is to know God, period, whatever your circumstances in life—rich or poor, strong or weak, famous or obscure. It is not that faith inspires you to work hard or raise a family or achieve your goals—though it very well might—but faith is its own reward also.

These days religious liberty is under assault. A lot of people think faith is just an odd, colorful mask for the ugly face of intolerance. I am not saying we should feel put upon. I mean, saints were thrown to the lions; by that standard, we have it easy. What I am saying is that we have to advocate for our faith. And we should defend religious liberty not just on material grounds—that is, because people of faith do good things, like give to charity or volunteer. We should also defend it on spiritual grounds—that is, because living out our faith gives us joy.

What people of faith understand is there is more to life than what we can see and hear. And there is nothing more life-changing than coming to know the Lord. Once you realize that there is a God and that He is good and that He loves you—not just humanity at large, but *you*, the person—you realize that you are not alone. You are not just a body. You are body and soul. And life is not just a tale "full of sound and fury, signifying nothing" (*Macbeth,* 5.5.27–28). Life is full of meaning. That is why prayer is so important. It is the hotline to heaven. And that is why we object when government restricts religious liberty: When faith is ruled out of bounds, then happiness itself is put out of reach.

If you need an example, look no further than the Little Sisters of the Poor. I believe they are doing a noble work. And yet the administration has been trying to force them to offer benefits that violate their beliefs. The sisters have tried to negotiate with the administration, and frankly, its response has shown a total misunderstanding of faith.

On their website, the sisters have a cartoon strip that illustrates the disagreement perfectly. A sister and a bureaucrat are debating the issue.

The bureaucrat says, "You offer the stuff you object to in your plan and we'll pay for it."

The sister replies, "Our concern isn't the cost but the morality."

The bureaucrat says, "No, we're offering to pay for it, so your conscience is clear."

The sister responds—in big, bold letters—"That's not the way it works."

They should not have to participate in any way in something that violates their beliefs—even if it seems like a formality.

But that's the problem: The administration seems to believe only in a material world, where the only stuff that matters is dollars and cents.

But that's a cold, unfeeling world to live in. And that's not the kind of country that our Constitution envisions.

Why is this even an issue? Because I actually think religious liberty is going to make a comeback—because there is a growing need for faith. Let me give you one example. Over the past four years, I've met with a lot of people struggling with addiction. Not everyone is the same, but what a lot of them will tell you is that they feel a deep, gnawing pain inside and they turn to drugs to escape it. Eventually, they realize the only way to escape the pain is to turn to God. So when I see people struggling with addiction—do they need the best medical care? Absolutely, yes. But a lot of them need something more.

For a lot of them, that pain stems from loneliness, from a feeling that no one loves them, that they don't matter. And it wasn't until I met some of them face to face that I realized we all feel that loneliness at some level. We all feel that distance from God. What is sin but a turning away from Him? We sometimes forget this because we're more comfortable. When you have a good-paying job or a happy family, it is tempting to think, "I don't do drugs. I don't commit crimes. I don't have it as bad as other people. I'm a good person."

That, of course, is the exact wrong way to think. It is the sin of pride.

It reminds me of *The Screwtape Letters* by C.S. Lewis, which I kept a copy of in my briefcase for years. Uncle Screwtape, a demon, is teaching a young devil how to turn a man to sin. At one point Screwtape says, "Catch him at the moment when he is really poor in spirit and smuggle into his mind the gratifying reflection, 'By jove! I'm being humble'" ([HarperCollins, 1996], 69). If you ask me, Screwtape could have been a great political consultant.

The point is, I believe it was my faith that brought me to this realization: We all are sinners. We all need God. So it is not enough to create more jobs or raise people's wages—though we should do that too. There is a spiritual void that we need to fill. Perhaps poverty is God's way of leading us to contemplate something higher. The way I see it, the fight against poverty and the need for religious liberty go hand in hand.

I'll close with this: When you meet people who have beaten addiction, most of them say, "It wasn't me, it was God." They know the true source of their success. In their struggles, they have to come know Him—and find happiness.

And now we've come full circle. Every good work is the work of God. It is His grace working inside us. And when you realize that, you not only lose your pride, you lose any sense of despair. I believe that's the meaning of true happiness—at least in this world. It is not a cheap thrill or temporary exuberance: It is a deep, abiding inner peace.

And what gives us that peace is coming to know God. That's what I think Aquinas was saying.

Please pray for me and all our elected officials that we may be instruments of God's will.

—Paul Ryan, Speaker of the House
May 2016

Introduction

GOD IS IN THE HOUSE

"America is great because she is good."

This statement, often attributed to Alexis de Tocqueville and frequently repeated by politicians throughout the twentieth century, inspires and dismays people today. In our time, we read it and wonder—is America still great? Is America still good? Our Founding Fathers were God-driven men who believed the hand of God guided them to establish this nation. Many Americans still feel personally grounded in the religious principles that inspired our forefathers to draft the Constitution, the Bill of Rights, and the Declaration of Independence. They yearn for leaders today who are driven by the same principles as our founders.

By stark contrast, the mainstream media paints current government leaders, particularly the United States Congress, with a black brush. In fact, given these portrayals, it might be difficult for the average citizen to believe that today's officeholders are anything like the Founding Fathers—leaders who believed in God and sought His assistance. Instead, we are fed a steady diet of reports that portray Congress members as corrupt, contentious, greedy, and immoral.

Fortunately, the true state of affairs is not as bleak as the media's one-dimensional coverage might lead us to believe. While a few members of Congress might fit this unsavory depiction, most of them do not. Many members of Congress are faithful believers in God who actively seek His assistance and inspiration as they serve the people of America. This book sets out to illustrate boldly what really goes on behind closed doors. Its purpose is to convince readers that God still indeed plays a role in guidance and direction as members of Congress seek His hand.

Within these pages are firsthand accounts, stories of profound faith and testimony, shared by the very men and women who serve in the hallowed halls of the United States Congress. This compilation opens to full view the hearts of currently serving and recently retired leaders, proving that they asked themselves—and God—profound questions in their decisions to run, and in how they fulfill their responsibilities in Congress. These questions include, What is a person with a strong faith in God and the Judeo-Christian values of the Bible to do in such a setting? How does one's faith affect one's running for office? How does a Christian know whether he or she is being led by God or by one's ego to run for office?

This book has been compiled with the goal of illuminating for the reader the lives of some of today's leaders from many different regions of our nation. Both Republicans and Democrats are represented, as no one party has a monopoly on faith.

Examples of faith today include individual members of Congress who turn to God on a daily (and sometimes hourly) basis for guidance on how to lead, how to vote, and how to respond to our nation's crises. One testimony involves the healing of a Congressman's wife and son after the physicians advised that only one or the other could live. Another testimony begins before the Congressman was conceived, when his father made a promise to God during World War II that would influence his faith throughout his life. Yet another testimony includes how a scant faith was cemented in a POW camp before a firing squad. Yet another shows how as a young man a future Congressman came to believe God knew him and had a purpose for his life.

These pages include accounts gleaned from the lives of friends of Congresswoman Virginia Foxx, who came in contact with these men and women who love God during her time at a regular Bible study group, and the weekly prayer breakfast within Congress brought her to know their hearts. Dr. Foxx soon came to feel that Americans deserve to know that they are being represented by people very different from the faithless caricatures presented by the modern media. With care and hope, she worked to collect these heartfelt and revealing stories to inspire a renewed optimism in Americans who care whether Bible values still matter in the lives of those who lead this country.

Each of the brief, inspiring testimonials that follow portrays "God moments" in the life and service—often the very decision to serve—of selected members and former members of Congress—in their own words.

Faith-seeking Americans will find in these moving stories a restoration of confidence in the goodness, and the greatness, of our Nation Under God.

Congresswoman

JANICE HAHN

DEMOCRAT—CALIFORNIA

FORTY-FOURTH DISTRICT (2013 TO PRESENT)

THIRTY-SIXTH DISTRICT (2011 TO 2013)

★

Religious affiliation: Churches of Christ

Birthdate and place: March 30, 1952; Los Angeles, California

Children: Three children, Danny, Mark, and Katy; five grandchildren, McKenna, Brooklyn, Isabela, Josiah, and Luke

Education: Abilene Christian University, Bachelor of Science in Education, 1974

"But a certain Samaritan, as he journeyed, came where he was: and when he saw him, he had compassion on him."

—Luke 10:33, KJV

★

The year was 1920. My grandmother Hattie Hahn was pregnant with her seventh boy, and her husband, John, was preparing to move from Canada to Los Angeles in the hopes that the climate would be better for his heart condition and his health. He found a house, sent for Hattie and their six little boys, and prepared to settle his family in a new land.

Tragically, before the move was complete, John Hahn succumbed to a heart attack. Hattie was left to grieve the loss of her husband alone, far from the rest of her family, with her six sons and a seventh on the way. To make matters worse, a relative had convinced her to let him invest her money, and then proceeded to embezzle all of it.

So there was my grandmother—destitute, a foreigner, and a single mother of seven boys under the age of ten, including her most recent son: my father, Kenneth.

Hattie had no visible evidence in her life that anything would change for the better, so in a moment of despair and hopelessness, she decided to end it all.

She took her seven young boys into her kitchen, taped the windows and door shut, and turned on the gas oven.

According to the story that was passed down in our family, she then felt the unmistakable presence of God and a reassurance that they would be alright and that her little boys would grow up to have special influence.

My grandmother must have had incredible faith, or maybe faith just the size of a mustard seed, because she believed God and turned off the gas.

Instead, she turned on a little radio in her kitchen and heard Aimee Simple McPherson preaching the gospel. She knew it was a sign, and she never looked back.

Those seven little boys grew up and were all very successful in their own ways. Some went into ministry, some into business, and my uncle Gordon and my dad went into politics.

I know for a fact that I am alive today because my grandmother didn't give up when things were dark and hopeless. I know I am here for a purpose. Although, I must admit I'm not always sure if I'm fulfilling that divine purpose.

I have devoted much of my life to public service and have tried to follow in the footsteps of my father. My dad was a Los Angeles County Supervisor for decades and became a beloved household name across Southern California. He was perhaps most well-known for a story about the day he met Dr. Martin Luther King Jr. It was the early 1960s, and Dr. King was visiting the LA area. During this time, politicians like Theophilus "Bull" Connor in Birmingham, Alabama, had approved the use of fire hoses and police attack dogs against civil rights activists and associates of Dr. King, including the children of protestors.

Many white politicians and government officials in other parts of the country, including Los Angeles, may not have acted like Mr. Connor, but they made their opinions clear by refusing to associate with Dr. King.

When the preacher of a local church called city officials in Los Angeles and asked if they would greet Dr. King at the airport with an official welcome, every one of them claimed to be busy. The preacher called the mayor, he called city council members, he called state senators, but every one of them had a "scheduling conflict." When he called my dad, my dad said, "I would be honored to greet Dr. King."

My dad went to Los Angeles International Airport with an official certificate of welcome from the County of Los Angeles and met Dr. King on the runway. He invited Dr. King for a ride in his own car and drove him around the city. My father represented Watts, a low-income, African-American neighborhood in southern LA, and he took Dr. King on a tour of the area. Then they returned to my father's office for a cup of coffee and began to talk about the future of this country. Dr. King shared with my father what his hopes and dreams were for America and the future of race relations. My father would later say he was the first one to hear the "I Have a Dream" speech.

After the Watts riots in 1965, my father worked to build a hospital in the heart of Watts because one of the findings in the McCone Commission, which looked at the root causes of the riots, was that there was a lack of accessible health care for people in south central Los Angeles. Then, in 1968, Dr. King was assassinated. My father called Mrs. King and said, "I know you don't know who I am but I'd like your permission to name this hospital in Watts after your husband." She said, "Actually,

I do know who you are. After my Martin met you, he couldn't stop talking about the white official who was so kind to him."

I love that story. Sometimes people wonder where I get my political courage and my feeling of what is right and what is wrong. This story of how my father lived his life tells it all.

After I had been in Congress a couple of months, Representative Mike McIntyre (D–North Carolina) invited me to attend a weekly bipartisan prayer breakfast held every Thursday morning at eight a.m. The occasion includes singing hymns, praying for one another, and hearing about a journey of faith from one member of Congress. I enjoy attending because when we are there, we do not talk politics, and we realize that everybody has the same issues in their lives. We all face personal and family problems. Many of us have close friends or family with health issues or other struggles. But I have found that when we pray for others, it breaks down the normal political barriers we have erected.

I think anything we can do to break down barriers and find common ground will lead to a better atmosphere in Congress, which, I hope, will lead to compromises and getting things done for the American people. That's what this country wants—for us to come together to solve problems.

A few years ago, Virginia Foxx (R–North Carolina) invited me to attend a women's Bible study on Wednesday mornings. She told me jokingly, "You'll attend if you know what's good for you." There, women from both sides of the aisle study the Bible together. I learn something new every week about the Bible, about my fellow Congress members, and about myself.

Both the weekly bipartisan prayer breakfast and my

women's Bible study help me to see and understand all sides and all views. I know Republicans and Democrats sometimes have differing views, in fact we see the world completely differently, but for me, these moments of shared prayer and faith remove the toxicity from the discussion and neutralizes the feeling that you must hate the other side and question their motives.

I remember once, several years ago, Representative Foxx had brought a group of people in for a tour of the Capitol. They were up in the gallery, and I was down on the floor. She pointed to me and said, "You see that women down there? She's a California Democrat. I don't agree with anything about her politically, but I really like that woman."

I don't go to prayer breakfast or women's Bible study for political reasons, but a couple of times I have had support on a bill or one of my amendments from some of the members who attend these weekly prayer meetings because we trust each other.

I want to continue to find ways to work across the aisle, to make friends, to build bridges, to find ways to compromise without sacrificing my deeply held principles, to do something positive for the people I represent and serve, and to make federal government work for everyone. I think that's what the American people want us to do.

I have three wonderful children and five beautiful grandchildren. They call me Mimi, and my annual Christmas card features my grandchildren on the front. One Christmas we posed in front of the United States Capitol. The inscription on the card read "Our Mimi goes to Washington." I am proud of my family, my children and my grandchildren. I am proud of my grandmother Hattie and of my father. I hope they are proud of me and my work too. At the end of the day, that's what you want—that your family can be proud of your work. And maybe that is the divine purpose that Hattie Hahn spared her family for.

Before being elected to Congress in a special election in July 2011, Janice Hahn served her community as a teacher, a business-woman, and as councilwoman in the Fifteenth District of the City of Los Angeles for ten years. Janice now serves the Forty-fourth District of California in the House of Representatives and sits on the Committee on Homeland Security, the Subcommittee on Counterterrorism and Intelligence, and the Committee on Small Business.

She is the recipient of the Rosa Parks Award from the Southern Christian Leadership Conference, the Lillian Mobly Grassroots Catalyst Award, the Public Service Award from the African-American Chamber of Commerce, the Bold Vision Award from the San Pedro Chamber of Commerce, and enshrinement on the Promenade of Prominence in Watts, California.

Former Congresswoman

SUE MYRICK

REPUBLICAN—NORTH CAROLINA

NINTH DISTRICT (1995 TO 2013)

★

Religious affiliation: Methodist

Birthdate and place: August 1, 1941; Tiffin, Ohio

Spouse: Wilbur Edward Myrick

Children: Two children and three step-children; twelve grandchildren, eight great-grandchildren

Education: Heidelberg College

"Take therefore no thought for the morrow: for the morrow shall take thought for the things of itself. Sufficient unto the day is the evil thereof."

—Matthew 6:34, KJV

★

I grew up in church. I went to Sunday school when I was little, then choir and youth group as I got older. There is always something going on in the church community, so I was very active. It was a very important part of my youth, and being spiritually involved has remained a very important part of my life.

It was my mom more than my dad who made sure I went to church regularly. My dad was one of those people who went to church on holidays. Both my mom and grandmother were very spiritual and instilled in me a sense of *spirituality,* as opposed to religion. Religion has caused a lot of problems in the world. But to be spiritual in one's life—that, to me—is different.

I never imagined I'd be involved in politics. It wasn't a career plan for me, or even a natural interest of mine. But when my husband and I encountered a challenge with the city of Charlotte, I started becoming more aware of what the city council did and how it controlled our lives. And so I volunteered, with no experience or money or anything, to run for Charlotte City Council. That was thirty-five years ago. The first time I ran in 1981 I lost by only two hundred votes. That gave me the confidence to run again; and the next time, I was elected. I have been in and out of politics since then.

In 1987, it became apparent to me that the Lord wanted me to run for mayor of Charlotte. I did not want to do it, but there was this little voice inside me that kept saying, "You need to run for mayor. You need to run for mayor." I know it sounds crazy to most people, but that's the only way I know how to describe it.

I finally gave in, and I ran just to be obedient to God. Polls indicated that I would not win, and I didn't think I would win. But what I did know was that He was asking obedience of me. It was a difficult, difficult race because there was a very popular incumbent in office. Charlotte was on a roll, and everyone said, "Everything is wonderful in Charlotte." People didn't feel the need for new leadership. I would constantly hear, "You are a nice person, but you don't stand a chance." And I would say, "I understand that, but I'm just being obedient to what I think God wants me to do." I won by a thousand votes, and that was the beginning. I knew He worked in all aspects of my life, but that's when I became aware of just *how* He was working in my life.

During my time as mayor, He brought people together in unbelievable ways. For example, Charlotte needed a homeless shelter, and we had been praying for one. One day somebody walked in to my office and said, "God has been very good to me, and I want to either give you $100,000 or renovate a homeless shelter for our city." He was a contractor. We said, "We'll take the work." He proceeded to get all of his subcontractors to donate their time and materials, and we got a homeless shelter built in Charlotte. It was a miracle. It was not me doing it, but it was God working through me as a vessel. Time and again, He brought people to me to make things happen.

I ran for the United States Senate in 1992 in a very ugly race. My opponent was a millionaire who used his own money to run, and he did everything he could to destroy me. It was a very bad experience. I decided that I did not want anything more to do with politics. Then, in 1994, our congressman decided—unexpectedly—to step down. Again, I did not want to go back into politics, and when asked, I simply said I was not interested in running. I became a bit frustrated with the pressure and finally said, "Well, do a poll and see how my negatives and positives are. You'll see that my negatives are so high from the Senate race that I couldn't get elected dogcatcher, and then you'll leave me alone."

So a poll was conducted, and it came back that my positives were very high and my negatives were very low. My husband and I thought about it, prayed about it, and decided that if we could give a few years of our lives for the future of our grandkids and try to help change the country that it was worth it. I was the last person in a five-person primary with no money—all the money was committed. Then, same story, I won again, and that's how I ended up in Congress.

We have a women's Bible study group in Congress, which is a wonderful thing. I started it eighteen years ago at the urging of then-Congressman (and later Senator) Tom Coburn (R–Oklahoma, 2005 to 2015). There were Bible study groups for male members of Congress, but not one for female members, so he said, "You need to start a women's Bible study." The group has met almost every Wednesday morning that Congress is in session since then. Those Wednesday mornings were grounding time each week for me—to bring us back to reality and what was really important in life. Our Bible study helped us to come together and pray together for the country. There was no political talk at all during Bible study. Instead, it was where we shared our lives and tried to support one another.

There have been times of crisis in my life when I had to rely completely on that prayer and support—like when I had breast cancer. I had to go through chemotherapy, and it was absolutely terrible. I was very, very sick, and I prayed to God, "Lord, thank you for this day. I know tomorrow will be a better one." That's the way I got through it. If I had a bad day, I thanked Him. If I had a good day, I thanked Him.

I was in office during my cancer treatments. The week of chemotherapy I would stay home. I would work the other two weeks, between treatments. Then, when I was in radiation therapy, I would fly back and forth to Washington. I would get up and go to the hospital every day at 7:00 a.m., then get on a plane and go to DC. I'd fly back to Charlotte every night. I did that for quite a while.

It was tough, but He got me through it, and He gave me the energy to do my job in the midst of it. I was very blessed, and it was really the best thing that could have happened to me. Being in the position that I was gave me the opportunity to be able to share my story with other people and to help empower women to save their own lives through early detection.

I feel very strongly that God works in the lives of each one of us if we are open to be still and listen. Too much of the time we are not open because we are too busy doing our own thing.

I try to stay open to Him and hear what He has to say. When I left Congress, I knew I would not run again. I didn't want to completely retire, but I didn't know what He had in store for me. I'd pray about it and say, "God, whatever your will is, just lead me," because I'm willing to do it. It's just the way I've lived my life the last thirty-five years.

I look at my time in office as public service—not politics. It is another way to serve God. Heaven knows that today there is a big need for people to give of themselves in public service, but it is not easy. We get attacked by the press, and there will always be someone who disagrees with you. I would just encourage people who are of strong faith to get involved in public service, so that they can help change things. People of faith will always be needed to help lead this nation, particularly during the challenges that our country will continue to face in the future.

Former Congresswoman Sue Myrick served as the first female mayor of Charlotte, North Carolina, for two terms and is the former president and CEO of Myrick Advertising and Public Relations. She served nine consecutive terms in Congress, from 1995 to 2013. During her tenure, she served as vice chair of the Committee on Energy and Commerce as well as on the Permanent Select Committee on Intelligence. Among other roles, Myrick—a breast cancer survivor herself—co-chaired the House Cancer Caucus.

Sue is known by her colleagues as a devoutly Christian woman, a devoted mother, grandmother, and great-grandmother. She grew up in church and remains steadfast in her faith as she relies on the Lord to guide her personal and public life.

Congressman

J. RANDY FORBES

REPUBLICAN—VIRGINIA

FOURTH DISTRICT (2001 TO PRESENT)

★

Religious affiliation: Baptist

Birthdate and place: February 17, 1952; Chesapeake, Virginia

Spouse: Shirley Forbes

Children: Four children, Neil, Jamie, Jordan, Justin

Education: Randolph-Macon College, Bachelor of Arts, 1974; University of Virginia School of Law, Juris Doctorate, 1977

“Jesus saith unto him, Go thy way; thy son liveth. And the man believed the word that Jesus had spoken unto him, and he went his way.”

—John 4:50, KJV

★

My story may be a little different from others you will read here. No single individual or person has molded me or caused me to be where I am. We have a lot of wonderful colleagues here who attend a Bible study every Wednesday morning, and that Bible study is the most important part of my week here, as it gives me an opportunity to meet and come to know those individuals. But my testimony and the events that have influenced my testimony actually began before I was even born.

During World War II, my father was drafted to go to fight for our country like a lot of other young men. He was nineteen when he married my mother, and three days later he was off to war and ended up in Normandy. Even though he was not in the first wave, he came right behind. His parents had given him a little pocket New Testament Bible. It had a metal cover on the front of it; I think the argument was that if you had it in your pocket and a bullet hit it, it would probably protect you. Somewhere in Europe, I don't know exactly where, as my father was guarding German prisoners after the Normandy invasion, he took the time to pull that Bible out and read it.

He made a promise to the Lord that if he got back home, he would have his family with him in church every Sunday. Now, a lot of GIs made a lot of promises, but he kept his.

And so when he came back and had three children—I have a brother and a sister—we had to be in church every single Sunday.

As children, we hated it, especially when we went on vacation or anytime we were out of town. One weekend, while camping on the Currituck Sound in North Carolina, my sister and I thought we had finally beat the system. Daddy had not packed any Sunday clothes, it was Saturday night, and he hadn't mentioned anything about going to church. The next morning he got up and went off early; we thought he had gone fishing. We had won! Or at least we thought we had.

About twenty minutes later he came driving down this dirt path towards the campground, and he had a preacher in the car with him to have church. A church service was held at that campground for the next thirty years. He never broke his promise. Because of my childhood experiences and our regular church attendance, I didn't have any of the big mountaintop or valley experiences that some people do.

I did, however, have a bedrock faith that I carried with me throughout my life. I had a mother and father who loved me, and we had the opposite of a dysfunctional family. I always prayed—I was just used to praying. I prayed to pass tests and in every challenging situation I encountered. It was a big part of my life. I prayed about jobs I would take. I prayed about the girl I would marry. As a result of my praying, the Lord showed me the right things to do and I really began to see the fruits of my spiritual upbringing and my prayer life.

Little did I realize how soon I would need all that prayer training. About eight weeks before our first child was expected to be born, my mother called and said that my wife, Shirley, was hemorrhaging and needed to be taken to the hospital immediately. Those were the days when the husband was not always present in the delivery room with his wife. As soon as we arrived, we were separated. The medical staff took Shirley away in a rush, and we were both pretty confused.

At some point, while I waited in one area of the hospital, and Shirley was being prepped for surgery in another area, a doctor or nurse told my wife that they would not be able to save both her and the baby; they would have to take the baby. She tried desperately to explain to the staff that she would not let them take the baby, that she needed to see me first. But her requests went unanswered until she spoke the magic words, "I just want you to know that my husband is a lawyer, and if you take this baby without him being here, he's going to take this hospital apart."

They immediately brought her out of the operating room and took us into this separate little room where we could be together. The doctor there was a very reputable obstetrician, and he looked at me and said, "We've got to take the baby—we can't save both of them." And then I looked at him with all of the maturity of a twenty-six-year-old kid and said, "Well, what's the problem?" I didn't know what else to ask.

He said, "She's hemorrhaging and we can't stop it."

I said, "It will stop."

He looked at me like I was crazy, and then he said, "I'll give you about five minutes."

We didn't feel there was anything else to do at that time except to pray. So I knelt down next to the stretcher, and we prayed that the Lord would stop the hemorrhaging. When the doctor returned, the hemorrhaging had stopped. He was surprised, to say the least. He looked at me and he said, "It won't last." And I said, "It'll last."

After they put Shirley in a room, he came back in and said, "I'll put her in here, but the moment the hemorrhaging begins again, we'll have to take the baby," and I said, "Well, it will not start again."

He came back in twice more, and about twenty minutes later he said to her, "I don't know what's happening here, but this baby is coming naturally. And we are going to let him come."

He was just beautiful, 5 pounds 4 ounces, but he was two months premature. They put him under oxygen.

Our prayers had been answered. But there were still more prayers and more guidance from the Lord to come. When my parents and Shirley's parents arrived at the hospital, I told them about the baby, and then I started walking across the hallway to go see Shirley and the baby. Suddenly, I stopped. Somehow, I could feel that something was wrong with the baby. Both sets of parents laughed and brushed it off, saying something like, "He thinks because he is such a good lawyer, he can now be a doctor." And I said, "No, no. Something is wrong with the baby."

I walked down to the pay phone in the lobby (of course this was before cell phones) and called the doctor who was going to be our pediatrician. The doctor was not on call because it was Memorial Day weekend, and so I called his nurse,

Minnie, who knew my wife very well. I explained to her that I just felt something was wrong with the baby.

She asked, "What is the resident doctor saying?"

"He says the baby is fine."

"What does the obstetrician say?"

"The obstetrician says the baby is fine."

"Well, Randy, I'm sure he's fine."

And I said, "Minnie, I don't ask for much."

"Do you want Dr. Toland to come look at your baby?"

"Yes." I knew there might only be a ten percent chance that something was truly wrong, but when it's your baby's life on the line, that's a big percent.

And so, a short time later, Dr. Toland came walking down the hallway, a young guy with long stringy hair and grease on his hands because he'd been in the middle of working on his car when Minnie had called.

"Let me look at the baby," he said. For about twenty minutes, he checked out my son in the nursery. When he came out to talk to me, he looked at me in a strange way.

I asked, "Well?"

His response was, "The resident thinks he's okay, and the obstetrician thinks he's okay."

"What do you think?"

"Well, let me put it this way, today's Friday. If they are right, you'll be taking your baby home on Sunday; if I'm right, your baby will be dead on Sunday."

"What do you think is wrong?"

"I believe he has congenital pneumonia," the doctor said. "They have done a test which is standard, but the problem is that test won't be back until tomorrow, and I think that will be too late."

"What can you do?" I asked.

And he said, "You can let me go ahead and start treating him, and there is a chance if we do that, he might live."

Without hesitation I said, "Go ahead and do it." He immediately began treating our baby, who got worse and was moved to the neonatal unit at King's Daughters Hospital.

Because of Shirley's condition, she was in too much pain to walk, so I was going between the two hospitals (which were connected by a hallway) to see them. When I arrived at Shirley's room early Sunday morning, she asked me to call all the churches in town and request that they pray for our baby. She said that the Lord had put it in her heart that we were not helpless, and that we could pray. People from churches all across the region began to pray for a little baby they had never seen.

The end result was that (on that day) the baby started getting better and better. However, he remained on a respirator and was still in critical condition with pneumonia, but he had a nurse with him twenty-four hours a day. About the ninth or tenth day, the doctors were telling us that if we couldn't get him off the respirator, it could do damage to his brain or to his eyes. So we literally prayed, "Lord heal this baby in a way that even the doctors will know that it is You and a miracle."

I picked up the phone to call the hospital to let them know I was on my way. The nurse who answered the phone said, "You won't believe what has happened. This little five pound one ounce baby [the baby had lost three ounces] reached up and pulled the tubes out of his mouth. We have never seen that happen before; he is drinking a bottle now, and he is going to be fine."

That reminded and confirmed for us once again that the Lord does answer prayers, and we have seen it over and over again in our lives. When we and the doctors were interviewed for a special program on the television show *The 700 Club,* the doctors even said, "It was a miracle." That baby, Jamie, is now thirty-seven years old and a minister of music himself.

As the teacher of an adult Sunday school for almost thirty years at my local church and founder of the Congressional Prayer Caucus, the necessity of prayer remains an integral part of my life, and I have seen the impact it has had in my life and the life our nation.

Congressman Randy Forbes is a devoted husband and father of four. A life-long resident of Virginia, Randy practiced at Kaufman & Canoles PC, one of the largest law firms in Virginia, before beginning his congressional career. He served the Commonwealth of Virginia as a member of the House of Delegates for seven years and in the Virginia Senate for three and a half years before being elected to the United States House of Representatives. He has earned numerous awards during his time in Congress, including "Guardian of Seniors' Rights" and "Hero of Taxpayers," and he serves on numerous committees. He is the founder of the Congressional Prayer Caucus, a bipartisan group of representatives and senators that work to protect prayer and our nation's spiritual history.

Congressman

SAM JOHNSON

REPUBLICAN—TEXAS

THIRD DISTRICT (1991 TO PRESENT)

★

Religious affiliation: Methodist

Birthdate and place: October 11, 1930; San Antonio, Texas

Spouse: Shirley Johnson (d. December 3, 2015)

Children: Three children, Bob, Gini, and Beverly; ten grandchildren

Education: Southern Methodist University, Bachelor of Arts in Business Administration, 1951; George Washington University, Master of Science in International Affairs

Military service: United States Air Force, 1950 to 1979

"It is of the Lord's mercies that we are not consumed, because his compassions fail not. They are new every morning: great is thy faithfulness."

—Lamentations 3:22–23, KJV

I grew up in Texas, going to church every Sunday. It was required. I didn't realize it at the time, but as an adolescent, I didn't really know the Lord or comprehend the breadth and depth of what it meant to fully submit your life to Him. It was much later in life and under horrific circumstances that I discovered He was with me throughout any situation, and only then did I come to truly know the Lord.

During the Korean War, I flew sixty-two combat missions in a plane I affectionately named "Shirley's Texas Tornado," so named for my two true loves—my wife, Shirley, and my beloved Texas. As a young and highly skilled officer and pilot, I had damaged one enemy plane and had logged one probable kill and one confirmed kill during my career, which gave me confidence in my own abilities.

My second tour of duty was Vietnam, and on my twenty-fifth mission, the enemy shot down my plane. It was April 16, 1966. Broken and battered from the low-level ejection while flying 650 knots, I felt terrible but still alert and eager to get out of enemy territory. Little did I know it was going to be a very long time—almost seven years—before I would embrace my wife and kids or experience the beautiful blessing of freedom again.

It was when I faced a firing squad on one of my first days

as a prisoner of war in North Vietnam that my realization of God's presence and protection became instilled within me. A captor told me in his attempt at broken English that I had been found guilty of trying to overthrow the North Vietnamese government, and they were going to take me out and shoot me—right now. Sure enough, they paraded me out in front of a firing squad of five soldiers carrying AK-47s.

As they blindfolded me, I started praying harder than I ever had before. I told God that I loved Him and I needed him, while also begging and pleading for His protection. When the commander yelled "FIRE" the only sound I heard was CLICK, CLICK, CLICK, CLICK, CLICK.

I still don't know what prompted me to do so, but I just laughed at them. After that, I wasn't ever afraid of them, because I knew He was with me. They then kicked me down into the slit trench and left me there. It has been said, "There is no such thing as an atheist in a foxhole," and the same could also be true of a POW camp.

Our captors forced us into silence as much as possible, so we used the old Smitty Harris Code to communicate by tapping on the walls. We used a 5x5 letter grid for the alphabet with five letters in each row and five letters in each column (skipping the k). Each letter was communicated by tapping two numbers: the first tap series represented the row number of the letter, and the second tap series designated the column number of the letter. The letter "A" would have been specified with one tap, a pause, and then one tap. Each night we would sign off with "GBU" for *God Bless You*. This small reminder of our faith was encouragement for each of us to cling to.

It didn't matter which Hanoi Hilton cell block we were in—nicknamed things like New Guy Village, the Zoo, the Heartbreak Hotel, or Las Vegas Village. Even though we couldn't often see each other, much less talk to each other, our adopted tap code allowed us to share a deep and abiding faith (and save our sanity). We encouraged one another as often as possible.

Because of my "die-hard resistance" against the North Vietnamese, I was separated from the others and moved into solitary confinement for forty-two months. Ten other POWs were also labeled "die-hards" and placed in separate cells. We called ourselves the Alcatraz Gang.

Towards the end of my time in the Hanoi Hilton, the North Vietnamese began to put larger groups of POWs in rooms together. Those of us in Room 7 agreed that we were sick and tired of missing Christmas with our loved ones, and we planned a church service. SRO Jim Stockdale requested permission to do so, but the Camp Commander denied us—twice.

Ignoring their warnings against it, we decided to conduct one anyway. One POW quoted Bible verses, and I sang hymns. Armed guards quickly arrived to break up this unauthorized and threatening meeting. After the guards escorted the ring-leaders out for more solitary confinement and brutal torture, our Medal of Honor recipient (Bud Day) burst into singing the National Anthem, "God Bless America," and other songs of that magnitude. Not only did the entire group in Room 7 chime in, but we were joined in succession by those in Rooms 6, 5, 4, 3, 2, and 1. We learned later that our songs of pride and defiance were loud enough to be heard outside the fifteen-foot walls of the Hanoi Hilton.

Faith was all we had, but it was a faith that was unstoppable. The fire lit within us during our church services inspired us to carry on with an even greater trust in the Lord.

Looking back on that time, I know that the Lord was with me. He helped me stay strong through those nearly seven years. He reunited me with my loving and praying family back home in Texas in February 1973. That homecoming will always be one of His greatest blessings in my life, and for that I will always be grateful.

Fast forward to my time in Washington. With a body broken by my captors but alive with the Holy Spirit, I can share a vivid testimony for Christ. Thanks to His handiwork, I have found it easy to make friends of faith on Capitol Hill. Through it all, one lesson still strikes clearly. The scriptures say, "We fix our eyes not on what is seen, but on what is unseen, since what is seen is temporary, but what is unseen is eternal" (2 Corinthians 4:18, NIV). I humbly thank God for every wonderful blessing in my life, including the blessing of *freedom* and that I can call America *home*.

Congressman Sam Johnson served twenty-nine years in the United States Air Force. A decorated combat veteran and war hero, Sam flew missions in both the Korean and Vietnam wars. He was awarded two Silver Stars, two Legions of Merit, the Distinguished Flying Cross, one Bronze Star with Valor, two Purple Hearts, four Air Medals, and three Outstanding Unit Awards. He endured nearly seven years as a prisoner of war in Hanoi during the Vietnam War;

almost half that time was in solitary confinement. He chronicles his captivity in his autobiography, *Captive Warriors.*

Following retirement from the Air Force, Johnson started his political career with service in the Texas State Legislature. He has served in the United States House of Representatives since 1991 and is currently a Deputy Whip, a member of the House Committee on Ways and Means, and Chairman of the Social Security Subcommittee, among other roles.

In 2009, he was voted most-admired Republican member of the US House of Representatives. That same year, the prestigious Congressional Medal of Honor Society awarded him their highest civilian accolade—the National Patriot Award—for his tireless work on behalf of the troops, veterans, and freedom. In 2016, he received the Patriot Award from the Bipartisan Institute.

Former Congressman

ALLEN WEST

REPUBLICAN—FLORIDA

TWENTY-SECOND DISTRICT (2011 TO 2013)

★

Religious affiliation: Christian

Birthdate and place: February 7, 1961; Atlanta, Georgia

Spouse: Angela West

Children: Two children, Aubrey and Austen

Education: University of Tennessee, Bachelor of Arts in Political Science, 1983; Kansas State University, Master of Arts in Political Science, 1996; United States Army Command and General Staff College, Master of Military Arts and Sciences, Political History, Military History and Operations, 1997

Military Service: United States Army, 1982 to 2004

"Have not I commanded thee? Be strong and of a good courage; be not afraid, neither be thou dismayed: for the Lord thy God is with thee whithersoever thou goest."

—Joshua 1:9, KJV

★

When I look back at where I have been throughout my life, including three different combat zones, a member of the United States House of Representatives, and where I am today, it is clear that God has ordered my steps. From 2005 through 2007—two and a half years—I was just a guy training the Afghan Army in Kandahar. Less than a decade later, I've served in Congress and now take up the cause of freedom as a political commentator and author. I often think about what it means to stand for right and what you have to go through to protect our freedoms. Isaiah 54:17 tells us "No weapon that is formed against thee shall prosper; and every tongue that shall rise against thee in judgment thou shalt condemn. This is the heritage of the servants of the Lord, and their righteousness is of me, saith the Lord." That verse hangs on my office wall to remind me of my duty as a servant of the Lord. Likewise, this verse in Philippians 4:13 has sustained me through my life: "I can do all things through Christ which strengtheneth me." That's how I tackle life.

I rely as much on the Lord today as I did on the battlefield and as I did as a member of Congress. You are supposed to trust in the Lord and lean not unto your own understanding. That's in Proverbs, and it is not just for big things, but it is for everyday things—it is part of a routine. When you do things routinely, you live a properly planned and executed life. So whether I'm in a combat zone, or on Capitol Hill voting on legislation, or praying for my daughters to be strong Christian women, I know from whence the source of the blessings come.

I was raised in a Christian home, and I read daily from a devotional while I worked in D.C. My devotional now is the book *In God We Still Trust.* It refers back to the faith convictions of the Founding Fathers and many of the great heroes in the history of this country.

I come from third- and fourth-generation military backgrounds. My father served in World War II, and my mother served at Marine Corps Headquarters in Atlanta, Georgia, as a civilian. My brother was a Vietnam-era Marine. I served twenty-two years myself. I have a nephew who is following in my footsteps a US Army major. My wife and I have been married for twenty-six years, and we have two daughters, twenty-three and nineteen, and even my wife is the daughter of a career military man as well.

I think it would be wonderful if every person chose a few critical Bible verses to memorize and use in their lives. For me, during trials and difficulties on and off the battlefield, I go to Romans 5:3–5 where it talks about trials and tribulations producing perseverance, and perseverance producing character, and character producing hope. I also enjoy Joshua 1:5–9, which emphasizes being strong and of good courage. These are the principles I have relied on to guide and carry me through life. They are principles I will continue to follow as God closes and opens the doors of my life.

Former Congressman Allen West served twenty-two years in the United States Army. West fought in Operation Desert Storm and Operation Iraqi Freedom; he was battalion commander for the Army's 4th Infantry Division. In Afghanistan, he trained Afghan officers to take on the securitizing responsibilities for their country. Upon retiring from military service, West taught high school in South Florida. He was elected to the United States House of Representatives in 2010 and served as a member of the 112th Congress.

He and his wife, Angela, have been married for twenty-six years and are the parents of two children.

Former Congressman

MARK CRITZ

DEMOCRAT—PENNSYLVANIA

TWELFTH DISTRICT (2010 TO 2013)

———★———

Religious affiliation: Catholic

Birthdate and place: January 5, 1962; Irwin, Pennsylvania

Spouse: Nancy Critz

Children: Two children, Joe and Sadie

Education: Indiana University of Pennsylvania, Bachelor of Science in Management Information Systems, 1987

"ARE NOT FIVE SPARROWS SOLD FOR TWO FARTHINGS, AND NOT ONE OF THEM IS FORGOTTEN BEFORE GOD?"

—LUKE 12:6, KJV

★

I will give you a history and then share my testimony. I worked in the office of Congressman John Murtha. He represented the Twelfth District of Pennsylvania for thirty-six years; but on February 8, 2010, he passed away suddenly. I highly respected Mr. Murtha and was grateful I had found a job I considered the best job I had ever had—helping people solve their issues or pointing people in the right direction. It was something I should have been doing all my life but didn't realize until I went to work for Mr. Murtha. I was happy as could be working for a member of Congress, doing what I could in the district.

When Mr. Murtha passed away there was a great deal of immediate apprehension, and as I was district director, the staff naturally looked to me for guidance. We were like family. In my mind, I thought, it'll work out. We'll figure out a way; a path will be set for us; it might not be the path we think—maybe a little rough, but we'll get there. . . . No one wanted to go public with any plans immediately after his death, but eight days after he was buried there were rumors going all around that Mrs. Murtha might run.

A number of people began announcing their intentions to run to fill out Mr. Murtha's term. Obviously none of the announced candidates could measure up to Mr. Murtha; but it wasn't my decision. My goal had never been to be a congressman; I was thrilled just to work in the office. During the next week I discussed my thoughts with others about how we were going to work this out. The chief of staff and I decided if Mrs. Murtha didn't run, we would support one of the people who had announced.

When I talked to Mrs. Murtha over the weekend, I learned she was not going to run. She asked me, "Have you thought about running?" I responded, "Yes, I have." It had been sort of a nagging thought, but right before my conversation with her, it hit me that I just had to do this.

I give God the credit, because I don't know where else to put the credit—and where else is there?

This wasn't something that I had ever planned in my entire life. I never thought in my wildest dreams that I would ever even consider running for Congress, but as I was going into that conversation with Mrs. Murtha, this huge weight came off my shoulders. I saw this path that I had to take.

The truth of the matter is—and this is why I'm compelled to give the credit to God—that it had nothing to do with me; it had nothing to do with me at all. This was about the people of the Twelfth District, the people of Pennsylvania, the people that had been served by Jack Murtha all these years. There were so many good things that had taken place, and I was a tool to continue the good work, to build on that, and to do good things for the people of Pennsylvania.

Mrs. Murtha said, "Mark, if you run, I'll support you."

From the moment of my decision to run, anything that needed to go right for me to get to Congress went right.

Things just went into place; there were things I didn't even think about that when they happened, I went "Oh."

For example, a former lieutenant governor who was going to run suddenly dropped out of the race and endorsed me without my ever talking to him. I thought, "Wow, that's amazing." Then it hit me that his endorsement was very strategic because I needed the support of a state committee to obtain the nomination. I knew none of these members, but the former lieutenant governor knew them all. So this endorsement was a big issue. He became a soldier, if you will, to help me win the statewide seat of endorsement.

Then there was a woman in the race who had won four statewide elections, serving two terms as Pennsylvania's Auditor General and two terms as the treasurer. She was well known as a campaigner; but the day after the petitions were due, she unexpectedly dropped out of the race.

I was continuing with the race, and there were just multitudes of things taking place. Every step I just kept walking by faith. This wasn't me, this was a path that had been laid before me, an opportunity to be helpful to my fellow countrymen, my fellow Pennsylvanians, and I was being called by a higher power. I wasn't just some politician that had thought about running all my life—I am on a mission. This is about serving the people of this country the best way I know how, and carrying forward God's principles: caring for one another, doing my best to lift people up, and carrying that belief through.

And so, what you'll find about me is that I'm not an overt person, I am not shy or introverted, but I am not overt in my faith. I practice diligently, but I'm not someone who has to prove it to people.

I know who I am. I know who I am in my heart, and that's all that matters. My feeling is, and has always been, that my entire life is led by example. I don't need to tell you that I truly believe in God and that this is where our power comes from and this is how we should have our mindsets and how we believe. I carry that conviction within me.

And so that's my story. In Congress what I did with every decision was to ask, "What are the emotional and social things we need to be doing to help our people when they need our help?" And "What are the things we are doing that maybe we shouldn't be delving into as a government?"

So that's how I got to Congress. As I went through the election, I was never tired, despite being up at five o'clock in the morning, going all day campaigning, and then answering emails until one in the morning. I had to quit my job to run, so for three months I went without a paycheck. Despite what should have been a burden, I kept feeling the same soothing reassurance: *Everything will be okay. You have to do this.*

After three months of working twenty-hour days, seven days a week, exhaustion finally overtook me on the Saturday night before the election. I lay down on the floor and slept for four hours because I just could not continue. I had become exhausted; I had carried myself for too long.

But the rest of Sunday, Monday, Tuesday, and the election turned out really well. Then, because it was a special election, I had to run again in November. Thankfully, I was successful there as well, even though things didn't go as "unexplainably smoothly" as they had months earlier.

I don't know what God's plan is. Perhaps I was needed in Congress to get me somewhere else. What I do know is that I couldn't deny the inner voice guiding me as I served.

I love my family. And one of the difficult parts of the job was being away from them. The job is taxing emotionally and demanded that I become much closer with God. Sometimes it's lonely on the Hill, and that's just the way it is. But I allowed God to show me the way, and I developed relationships across both parties.

Just like in any job, people can sometimes lose their way, even—maybe especially—on Capitol Hill. But I followed Mr. Murtha's example, remembering who I am and why I was there. Mr. Murtha always said that we are put on this earth to make a difference. That is what drove him, and what I hope drives me. I learned that most of the people in Congress want to do good things, to make a difference. And I truly believe that the desire to make a difference is driven by God.

From the outside, it may look like members of Congress disagree on nearly everything. But, really, there are compromises and efforts to agree ninety-nine percent of the time. It's just that the one percent of the time disagreements do occur, the media are right there to spread the news—it's how they make their money. I believe most of the people in Congress are doing their best to help this country to be as God-like as it has always been, but I think people get lost, and there are some people with the Congress and there are some staff members who work for Congress that view the work as only a job, not a calling from God to make a difference.

When I would drive in to work, I'd take New Jersey Avenue, and the first thing I'd see was the dome of the Capitol. I was in awe every time I realized I worked there. But then my inner voice would remind me that this was a huge responsibility, that I'd need that strength to make good decisions. I know not everyone in Congress feels as I felt, but I have hope that our country will not cease to be one driven by Christian principles. Faith in God and in each other can help us stay the course, while making the progress needed to keep this country great.

Former Congressman Mark Critz was born and reared in Irwin, Pennsylvania, and married his wife, Nancy, on September 5, 1987. They are the proud parents of twins. Among his numerous awards, he is the recipient of the highest civilian award issued by the National Guard Association of the United States—the Patrick Henry Award.

During his three years in Congress, Mark served on the Armed Services and Small Business committees. He was a member of the Military Families Caucus, the Rural Education Caucus, and the Arts Caucus, among others.

Former Congressman

STEVE SOUTHERLAND II

REPUBLICAN—FLORIDA

SECOND DISTRICT (2011 TO 2015)

★

Religious affiliation: Christian

Birthdate and place: October 10, 1965; Nashville, Tennessee

Spouse: Susan Southerland

Children: Four children, Samantha, Stephanie, Ally, and Abby

Education: Jefferson State Community College, Associates Degree in Mortuary Science, 1989; Troy University, Bachelor of Science in Business Management, 1987

"AND THE THINGS THAT THOU HAST HEARD OF ME AMONG MANY WITNESSES, THE SAME COMMIT THOU TO FAITHFUL MEN, WHO SHALL BE ABLE TO TEACH OTHERS ALSO."

—2 TIMOTHY 2:2, KJV

★

I was born in Nashville, Tennessee, while my parents were in college. My mom and dad were from Panama City, Florida, and we moved back there soon after I was born. Although I never lived in Tennessee, I still travel to those Smoky Mountains to get centered, decompress, and count my blessings. It's just an incredible place to visit.

I was raised in a Christian home where attending church was important and faith was suffused in our daily lives. We believe in a personal relationship with Christ, and as a result of my parents' influence, we believe that we will spend eternity together. I vividly remember the day of October 5, 1971, when I was almost six years old, kneeling down and asking Jesus Christ to come into my life. That day I submitted to His authority. It is a precious memory in my life and, still today, I find that I stand tallest after I have been kneeling before Him.

The same year that I accepted Christ I also met my future wife, Susan. We sat together in our first grade classroom and have been with one another ever since. Our families went to church together, and we participated in community activities together. We are equally yoked. She is my best friend and closest confidant, and being away from her and the kids was the hardest thing about serving in Congress.

As a result of growing up in a family that nurtured faith

and the basics of Christian living, I came to understand that God wants your full devotion. I understand that accepting His call is not about fun or pleasure, it's about obedience. In an obedient life, one experiences disappointment and elation, valleys and mountaintops. However, an obedient life leads to an abundant life.

Our home was like a recreation center. There were hundreds upon hundreds of Bible study meetings in our home. Heaven knows how many young men and women accepted Christ under the roof of the place I called home.

At the age of fourteen, I had a pivotal experience that shaped the rest of my life. As the result of a near-fatal baseball accident, we discovered that I had a calcium deficiency and could not continue to play baseball, a game that had become part of my identity. After I suffered months of depression and struggled to come to grips with my situation, my father came to me one day and said, "Son, I can't watch you do this anymore. We have to get this straight." So we knelt in prayer and asked God to help me come to grips with this change in my life. We prayed that God would take away my desire to play baseball, knowing that He will never take anything from us unless He has something remarkable for us in its place.

I believe that God does not wish for us to stay in the boat; rather, He wants us to climb over the edge and walk on water with Him in faith—knowing that He will never forsake us. Little did I know at the time of my accident that my father was paving the way for me to understand what it is like to step out of the boat and walk on the water. That was a critical learning experience and is still very emotional for me to discuss.

Telling that story gives me an opportunity to share an example of how critical marriage and parenting are to the family and how God's plan for the family is eternal and perfect in every way. My life shows that I'm the beneficiary of that plan.

I've learned that God is not as concerned with my comfort as He is with my obedience. We must offer ourselves up each and every day to His will. As I lived through that experience when I was fourteen, I prayed that God would take away my desire and remove that agonizing pain. God answered my prayer, and, over a few years, His plans for me were revealed. I believe He has a plan for everyone, and I believe that He has a plan for this nation. I think His hand is still on this nation, and I think it causes Him great pain when we deny Him. He wants to heal our land. He wants this nation to be a shining city. But He also desires that it be a city that burns bright because of our ability to deny ourselves to take up our cross daily and to follow Him—and that is why I served in Congress.

While there—and still today, of course—I was very unapologetic about my faith; it has been critical to my direction, and it is the compass of my life. As I got through my high school years and began to pursue other things—music, golf, and such—He began to bless me and began to give me gifts. I was student body president of my high school, which honed my leadership skills. In college, I played golf, was on a leadership scholarship, and was involved in the student ministry there, which taught me the importance of discipleship (2 Timothy 2:2)—the Master's plan of evangelism. Through intense discipleship, a group of about twelve of us became a band of brothers. We could turn to one another, we could share, and we could pray together. We became accountable to each other and we set standards for ourselves. We were called the "Troy Boys" because we attended Troy State together and remain close today.

During those college years, I spent a summer on the foreign mission field in the Philippines, and I did other summer missions throughout my college experience. I was constantly seeking God's will for my life, and He did, indeed, begin to reveal to me my career path. It was also His will that Susan and I would be partners for life.

Susan is my best friend, is an incredible wife for me, and a wonderful mother for our four daughters. Hopefully, we have passed on the same principles we were raised with—of faith and family and a commitment to God's Word. We are not perfect, but we do understand the standard.

We have followed my parents into our family-owned business—a funeral service which is sometimes intense and requires time and commitment, but which we also see as a ministry opportunity. We feel we are most effective in our business when we are most committed to the principles outlined in God's Word. We have an opportunity to be a Good Samaritan every day, and, as Jesus did when He looked upon the multitudes and was moved by compassion, we try do the same.

I believe in working hard! Work was in the Garden before the Fall. God has always expected work of His people, that they be strong, that they be courageous, and that they labor in the field. God's principles may seem difficult to follow day in and day out, week in and week out, but after a lifetime, year after year, decade after decade, you really begin to see the trajectory of an abundant life earned from following those daily principles.

I brought this mindset to Congress. I missed my family and my business while I was in Washington. I missed my group of accountability partners, but God had sent me on a journey—His journey. During my four years on the Hill, I prayed that He would raise up other members of Congress to join with me in His work, for the words of Matthew 9:37–38 to come to fruition: "The harvest truly is plenteous, but the labourers are few; pray ye therefore the Lord of the Harvest, that he will send for labourers into his harvest."

And God has raised up other members of Congress to be harvesters with me. Virginia Foxx, Jim Jordan, Tom Graves, Tom Price, and many, many other individuals I cherish and value from my time on the Hill. They are the people God brought into my life to give me a simple relationship of accountability, to challenge me, to hear my confessions, to partner with me in the harvest, and to be faithful to the principles that brought me there.

And so my time in Congress was really just more of the same routine from my earlier life and my current life; it was just a different place to be faithful to the principles that I have committed to in my life.

There are several verses that are very important to me, one of which is Galatians 2:20: "I am crucified with Christ: nevertheless I live; yet not I, but Christ liveth in me: and the life which I now live in the flesh I live by the faith of the Son of God, who loved me, and gave himself for me." I hope the same can be said of me. I want to be faithful, and I find that we must fight for our cause. Another is 2 Timothy 1:7, "For God hath not given us the spirit of fear; but of power, and of love, and of a sound mind." I believe the Founding Fathers followed principles based on these Words. As I study their lives, I have no doubt that the Judeo-Christian God of the Bible was the God they worshipped, and was the God they submitted their lives to.

George Washington was very clear in his belief that the God whose steady hand led the children of Israel out of Egyptian bondage is the same God whose steady hand was guiding the formation of this great nation. (See Michael and Jana Novak, *Washington's God* [NY: Basic Books, 2006].) Washington referred to God as Providence. I believe with all my heart that His hand is that same steady hand that we must turn to today to get us through these most difficult of challenges that we face.

It is my prayer that God continue to assemble men and women in the Capitol who (in their previous lives) have established a relationship with that same steady Hand. That those on the Hill who believe, will turn to Him once again for direction, for comfort, for strength, and for protection as they move this nation forward for our children and our posterity.

I believe that our best years are ahead for this nation. But I also believe that our future will be only as good and as bright as our commitment to the principles outlined in His Word. If God's people, who are called by His name, will humble themselves and pray, He will hear our prayers, and He will come, and He will heal our land, as promised in 2 Chronicles 7:14.

I served in Congress with that hope, that understanding,

and that expectation. But I was not alone. Many on the Hill are there in that same pursuit. I had wonderful examples to follow from legislators I worked with. Obviously there is evil, and there are people in Congress—as there are everywhere—who don't believe in these principles and want to pursue something that is more humanistic in form, and so you hear, "Washington is broken," and "Washington as a community is an evil place." I know of no place on the planet that does not have the ability to become an evil place. But I also know that God is there, in Washington—without question.

After voting on the floor on the first night of every week, I would go off to a little room and pray. Usually around twenty members were there—praying for America. We prayed for real people with real hurts and real hopes. There is a Bible study that I enjoyed attending when able. It was a true expository study, and I enjoyed it very much. It recalibrated me going into each week. Prayer recalibrated many of us.

I am encouraged by what I saw in the midst of a place that is sometimes very discouraging. That is the way God plans it. He equips those He chooses with everything that is necessary to bring light and salt to Washington, DC.

There are times when believers must make unpopular decisions, whether it's in Congress, the corporate office, or their own homes. Being a believer means you choose God's Way and not man's way. In April 2011, for example, I chose to vote no for a bill that came up on the floor. It did not move in a direction that I believed God wanted me to move. But I was very respectful of members who voted opposite of me; I didn't question their motives, and I didn't question their understanding of what we should do. In turn, they respected my reasoning.

In parenting, I think you make decisions all the time that are unpopular with your children as you give them direction. You set the boundaries, saying here are the boundaries for our home and the boundaries of our expectations, and they are not to be crossed or broken.

I come from a boating area in Panama City, Florida, and we have channel buoys. Channel buoys are there to keep your boat off rocks, to keep you off the sandbar, and if you honor those you stay in deep water. When you violate those buoys, the boat is not doing what the boat is intended to do. It's the same in life, as with a boat. We each have abilities and we each have values. For me, there are six clearly defined values: respect, discipline, excellence, honesty, courage, and loyalty. These buoys (boundaries) will help get me to my destination; but if I violate the buoys, then I get out of the channel, and my ship (my life) ends up on a sandbar, and I am not being productive. Boundaries are good. They are there to help us be productive and accomplish the mission for which we have been called.

I believe with all my heart that all things work together for good to those who love God and are called according to His purpose. I also believe that He is able to supply all of my needs according to His riches in glory. He will supply all my needs as long as I am about His purpose (like a ship). No king would send a ship on a mission flying the king's flag without having supplied in the hull of that ship all of the resources necessary to fulfill the king's mission.

As long as I am navigating through the waters on which He has sent me, towards the mission on which He has sent me, properly managing the resources within that hull, then I will accomplish the mission of the King. I will safely return home. I must constantly be in touch with the King; to fly His flag; to manage the resources that He has given me; to navigate the waters of life, to honor the boundaries of the buoys, and to stay off the rocks, and to be true to those values, to accomplish the mission—to return safely home.

Former Congressman Steve Southerland has been a lifelong Christian leader. He grew up in a family that owns and operates a third-generation small business in Florida, where he worked before his election to the 112th Congress. Steve also worked as chair of the Bay County Chamber of Commerce, was a member of the Economic Development Alliance, chair of the Early Learning Coalition of Northwest Florida, and worked with the Covenant Hospice Foundation Board. In Congress, he served on the House Committees on Agriculture, Natural Resources, and Transportation.

He is currently co-owner/president of Southerland Family Funeral Homes. He and his wife, Susan, met in the first grade and are now the parents of four children.

Congressman

STEPHEN FINCHER

REPUBLICAN—TENNESSEE

EIGHTH DISTRICT (2011 TO PRESENT)

★

Religious affiliation: United Methodist

Birthdate and place: February 7, 1973; Memphis, Tennessee

Spouse: Lynn Fincher

Children: Three children, John Austin, Noah, and Sarah

Education: Crockett County High School

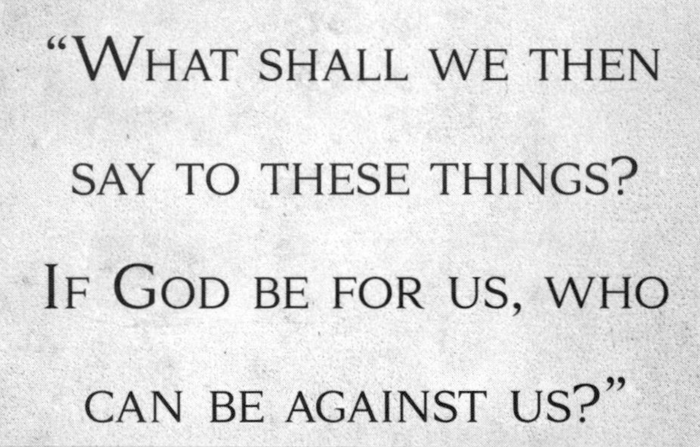

—ROMANS 8:31, KJV

★

I live in a small community in western Tennessee in a place called Frog Jump. We are a community of about four hundred people, and Crockett County is my home county. It is a very small county, without a single stoplight or Walmart in the whole place.

Like my father before me, I'm a cotton farmer—seventh generation. Fincher Family farms has been around Frog Jump for more than 140 years. For the past sixty years, the Fincher Family has been traveling the state in a gospel music singing ministry. I joined when I turned nine and have been singing baritone and playing bass with my father, uncles, and cousins ever since.

My wife, Lynn, and I have been married twenty-five years and have three children, John Austin, Noah, and Sarah.

Before running for Congress in 2010, I'd never been in public office. I had helped a couple of candidates financially, but had never held office myself. Life had always consisted of three things: taking care of my family, farming, and singing gospel music. Then in June of 2009, I was in the cotton field working spring cotton, and a business partner of my family called me. I'll never forget it. He said, "Stephen, have you been watching the voting record of our congressman?" We'd never had a Republican congressman hold this seat. Davy

Crockett was once the Congressman for this district and ran as a Whig—the closest thing to a Republican—back in the late 1800s. I admitted that I hadn't been paying attention. My partner responded that our representative was not voting the way we believed represented the area. He suggested that we find someone to run against him and thus change the way we were being represented.

I did not know where the conversation was going because we had never even talked about this and, furthermore, I was in the middle of a cotton field on a turn row in my big John Deere self-propelled sprayer on my cell phone. "Nobody can beat John Tanner," I told my friend. "He's got a million dollars in the bank. He's been there twenty years. He is pretty well liked in the district."

"Well, you could beat him," he said.

I replied with the only reasonable thing I could think to say: "You're crazy! This is nonsense. I don't know what you've been drinking, but friend, I am *not* running for Congress. I am happy here on the farm."

But he was relentless. He had a couple of friends in Jackson, Tennessee—the second-largest town in our district—that he wanted me to meet. I told him quite bluntly, "I really think this is a crazy idea. I don't have time for this."

"Well, we are business partners," he said. "And I want you to go meet with them and if you don't go, I won't be business partners with you anymore." And he kind of laughed.

Within a short time, I had met with Jimmy Wallace, who was very active in the Republican Party both here and in Jackson, and Tommy Hopper, who is my consultant now and actually lives in Jackson. We talked for three hours on our first meeting.

Tommy Hopper was the youngest state party chairman Tennessee had ever had. I told them that day, "Guys. I'm honored that you would think of me to do this, but I am *not* going to do this. This is crazy! I love the party, but they said I would have to raise two million dollars, and I can't raise money, and I'm not going to do this."

I got up to leave and (I'll never forget this) I grabbed the door handle, and I said, "I'll tell you what I will do—I will pray about this, me and my family."

I'm a Methodist; I go to a small Methodist church in Frog Jump. My great-great-grandparents on my dad's side donated the land to build on, and on my mom's side gave the lumber to build with. There is a very deep history with my family and our church, and our faith, which is very important to me.

I left that day and came home to my wife who was cooking dinner. As I walked in, I told her, "You won't believe what's happened." And she said, "What?" I said, "I met a couple of guys today, in Jackson who want me to run for United States Congress."

As a husband and wife we've been through a lot together. She turned around and said, "Well, I'll tell you what will happen." I thought she was going to say, "You'll win" or "You'll do great" or something like that, but she said she would divorce me.

"If you do this," she said, "I will take the house, I will take everything. You will live in a box. I am not a politician's wife." And I said, "Whoa, whoa, whoa, just wait a minute. I think this is crazy, but the country is not going in the right direction. I don't think that I am the right person either, but for some reason or something, this has happened, so just pray about it. We will not talk about it anymore."

Ten days passed, and we did not talk about it anymore, but I had been in deep prayer about it. Something was stirring within me, but if my wife was not on board, then I would not do it because it was too much of a sacrifice.

One night I was doing the farm budgets. We run a large farm and it gets pretty complicated. My wife came into my office and sat down in front of me, and started crying—more like weeping. She is just beautiful. (I married way up.) As someone who has been married for twenty-five years, I have made a lot of mistakes, and so I started apologizing and she interrupted, saying, "No, no, no. You have not done anything wrong this time. It is this political thing. I did not want to do it, but we have to do it."

I knew already that something was happening, and when she told me that, I knew we had to take the journey. Now I was praying and seeking God and asking the question, "Am I going to win? Am I going to win?" I am competitive, and I wanted to win. I was running against somebody who had never been seriously challenged or beaten. One night I couldn't sleep and was up at about two o'clock in the morning, and I was reading Proverbs in the Bible, and I was just trying to get an answer or come to a decision, when God spoke to me (not a voice but in my Spirit), and He just said, "You've got to run." And I said, "Am I going to win?" And He said, "You've got to run."

So we started raising money. It's either a curse or a blessing, but I am an aggressive fund raiser because I think the country is at stake, and this is about my children, and our future, and I don't have anything to lose, but the country does. I raised about $350,000 in the first four weeks and kept going to raise about $700,000 in six months, and then Congressman Tanner decided to retire the first day of December. When he did that, two Republican doctors jumped in to the race and spent six million dollars combined to run against me, while I spent about one million. It was the most expensive primary race in the entire country. We won with 49 percent of the vote; they got 25 percent apiece.

Then we had a tough general election against a twenty-four-year state senator, but we also did well, and we won by twenty points. I love people, so I love serving and representing people, but the general job is just really, really hard. I want to get things accomplished for our future and our country, but everything in Washington is so political, and you've got politics on both sides of the aisle that are guiding decisions that shouldn't be guided by politics, so it has been so frustrating for me as someone from the private sector, but I've been on a remarkable journey. God has opened up so many doors.

My second year in Congress (2011) was probably the worst year of my life, even though I was more content than I'd ever been—and while that doesn't make any sense at all, what it means to me is that I'm doing what I'm supposed to be doing. I still have a part in the farm at home. I love home, and I love the farm. I farm every weekend, and I still sing gospel music every weekend, and I give the children's sermon at my church every Sunday morning. I am just so thankful that He has allowed me to do the things He has enabled me to do and to make the journey while still keeping my roots.

Now let me throw this in. I guess it was probably August 2009 (after we had been raising money for a while) that I was convinced I needed to make the complete journey, I needed to try. Kevin McCarthy (R–California), who is now Majority Leader in the House, and Lynn Westmoreland (R–Georgia) wanted to meet me in Nashville, so my wife and I went to Nashville for the meeting. I didn't know either representative from Adam, but I knew of their influence.

Before the meeting, I told my wife, "If they don't think I'm the type of material needed to serve, then I will transfer the money to someone else or give it back, so that someone else can run who can better fill the position. I want to do what is best for the district."

As I came into the meeting, my wife and I sat down, and I couldn't stop thinking about Kevin McCarthy as a beach boy from California who wouldn't know anything about Tennessee or cotton farming. Lynn Westmoreland, a Southerner from Georgia, who talks like me, would be more my type. We were talking around the table (McCarthy seated on my right, and Westmoreland across the table from me), and I'll never forget it: Kevin looked at me and said, "So, you're a farmer?"

"Yeah, yeah I am," I said.

And he said, "Well, what kind of cotton do you grow?"

Assuming that Kevin didn't know up from down (because we sometimes give a hard time to our colleagues from California), I said, "Well, Mr. McCarthy, I grow white cotton."

He laughed and then filled me in about the different

grades of cotton grown in California. We hit it off from that moment on.

And, of course, I did run. And I've found great men and women of faith here in Congress who likewise feel called to help our country. Representatives McCarthy and Westmoreland were two of the first.

I attend Bible Study when I am here in DC. We have a little prayer meeting and Bible study on Wednesday mornings. There are probably fifteen or twenty of us, and we just rotate offices. I don't go every Wednesday, but I go a lot of Wednesdays. I've had it in my office five or six times. It helps a lot.

If it weren't for the good people here in Congress with me—people who believe in God and want to let Him lead them—I would quit and go home. But a lot is at stake here—my children's future is riding on it—and our country needs God, and His followers, to keep America great.

Congressman Fincher serves on the House Committee on Financial Services, the Financial Institutions and Consumer Credit subcommittee, and the Oversight and Investigations subcommittee. He is also a member of the Committee on Agriculture. His seat was once held by frontiersman and politician Davy Crockett; Fincher is the first Republican since Crockett to occupy the seat.

Fincher is a seventh-generation managing partner of a West Tennessee-based agribusiness; he grew up learning the family business and is a staunch advocate for small businesses. He and his wife, Lynn, have three children.

Former Congressman

FRANK WOLF

REPUBLICAN—VIRGINIA

TENTH DISTRICT (1981 TO 2015)

★

RELIGIOUS AFFILIATION: Presbyterian

BIRTHDATE AND PLACE: January 30, 1939; Philadelphia, Pennsylvania

SPOUSE: Carolyn Wolf

CHILDREN: Five children, sixteen grandchildren

EDUCATION: Pennsylvania State University, Bachelor of Arts in Political Science, 1961; Georgetown University Law Center, Juris Doctorate, 1965

MILITARY SERVICE: United States Army Reserve, 1962 to 1967

"For I was an hungred, and ye gave me meat: I was thirsty, and ye gave me drink: I was a stranger, and ye took me in: Naked, and ye clothed me: I was sick, and ye visited me: I was in prison, and ye came unto me."

—Matthew 25:35–36, KJV

★

I was raised in a Christian home, and my faith evolved, if you will, as I grew. I can't say there was one particular moment that solidified my faith. Rather, it was a developmental process. I was already a believer when I came to Congress; and my faith increased dramatically during my thirty-four years there. The bipartisan Bible study group that has met since 1982 had a particularly significant impact on me.

Early on in my career on the Hill, I traveled to Ethiopia in an effort to learn more about the massive struggle with famine and hunger in the area. Christian aid agency World Vision let me join them in 1984 at relief camp Alamata. What I saw stunned me: thousands upon thousands of Ethiopians starving in squalid conditions, their eyes sunken and abdomens swollen. That trip changed me, awakening me to the suffering of others. The following year, I visited Cold-war era Romania, again taken back by the number of suffering and oppressed people in the country. I felt called to make these people—the poor, the hungry, the prisoner, and the oppressed—my mission.

Ecclesiastes 4:1 reads: "Again I looked and saw all the oppression that was taking place under the sun: I saw the tears of the oppressed—and they have no comforter; power was on the side of their oppressors—and they have no comforter" (NIV).

This is how I felt after my trip to Ethiopia and what has driven me to take every trip since. It is, quite frankly, what kept me in Congress so long, the desire to bring comfort—and sometimes power—to those who suffer. It is a cause we must continue to fight for, one that we must promote as we select new men and women to represent us in Congress.

I have seen God's hand in my life as I've met and worked with dozens of people throughout the world who follow Jesus. I am friends with a woman in Egypt named Mama Maggi. Her faith is indestructible despite difficulties that can arise from being a Coptic Christian in an Arab country. I had another friend, Shabaz Bhatti, who was a member of the cabinet in Pakistan. We became friends after I met him at a prayer breakfast in London and worked with him on several occasions. In March 2011, he was gunned down and killed because of his faith. In an interview given a month before his assassination, he said he was willing to die for Christ, and that's what he did—he died for Christ.

I met many giants of faith in Romania, where the church was greatly persecuted. Paul Negruts, Pastor of the Second Baptist Church of Oradea, met with me on my first visit to Romania in 1985, and many times since then. He was a leading person speaking out about the oppression of the Ceaucescu government and had received death threats for his outspoken faith. Another person I met with over the years, after he left Romania, was Father George Calciu, who had spent many years in prison in Romania. These giants were not deterred in their mission to alleviate suffering. I saw this same type of compassion in Russia and China during my travels. I have worked for many years with Bob Fu, after he left China; he is a pastor who now heads China Aid, a group in the United States that promotes religious freedom in China.

Throughout the world today, people are being persecuted for their faith more than at any time in the last one hundred years. The suffering is particularly intense for Christians in Iraq, where, ironically, more Biblical activity has taken place than in any other country in the world, with the exception of Israel. The events in the book of Esther took place in the area now called Iraq. Burial sites for several ancient prophets, including Ezekiel, Jonah, and Nahum, are found in Iraq. The great cities of Nineveh and Babylon were also located in Iraq, as was Ur, where Abraham was called up from God to serve him. Modern-day Christians in the area, despite intense persecution, are very committed; their faith is as deep as their Biblical roots.

We in the West, who can be relatively comfortable in our religious pursuits, would do well to remember our fellow Christians in Iraq and other areas of the world. Their faith is exemplary; their drive to help others who are suffering is powerful. We must do more to comfort the oppressed, to reverse the situation observed by the Preacher of old in Ecclesiastes, and return power to those willing to help the oppressed, the poor, and the hungry.

Former Congressman Frank Wolf is a hero to the ignored and forgotten martyrs of Christianity. During his thirty-four-year tenure in Congress, Wolf visited Ethiopia, Sudan, Sierra Leone, the Democratic Republic of the Congo, Rwanda, Lebanon, Algeria, Iraq, Afghanistan, Pakistan, Jordan, Syria, Egypt, Israel, and others in an effort to bring aid and comfort to those who suffer. He is a staunch advocate for global human rights.

Wolf served on the Appropriations Committee, was co-chairman of the Tom Lantos Human Rights Commission, and chairman of the Appropriations subcommittee on Commerce, Justice, Science and Related Agencies, where he was vital in forming anti-gang task forces. In 2011, Wolf published *Prisoner of Conscience: One Man's Crusade for Global Human and Religious Rights*, which chronicles his efforts.

Currently he is a Distinguished Senior Fellow with the 21st Century Wilberforce Initiative, and he holds the Jerry and Susie Wilson Chair in Religious Freedom at Baylor University.

Congressman

JUAN VARGAS

DEMOCRAT—CALIFORNIA

FIFTY-FIRST DISTRICT (2012 TO PRESENT)

★

Religious affiliation: Catholic

Birthdate and place: March 7, 1961; National City, California

Spouse: Adrienne Vargas

Children: Two children, Helena Jeanne and Rosa Celina

Education: University of San Diego, Bachelor of Arts in Political Science, 1981; Fordham University, Master of Arts in Humanities, 1987; Harvard Law, Juris Doctorate, 1991

"'Lord, when was it that we saw you hungry and gave you food, or thirsty and gave you something to drink?' . . . And the king will answer them, 'Truly I tell you, just as you did it to one of the least of these who are members of my family, you did it to me.'"

—Matthew 25:37, 40, NRSVCE

★

Years ago, as young twenty-somethings, on a trip deep in Mexico proper, a friend and I watched as a group of three boys boarded our second-class bus at 2:30 in the morning. Second-class busses travel long distances for cheap fares and often stop in the middle of nowhere if someone on the route happens to be hailing a bus, so it wasn't out of the ordinary for three passengers to stumble onboard in the middle of the night. In many cases, a new arrival would quickly be acknowledged and time would go on. But this night—and those boys' arrival—had an extraordinary outcome.

Right away, one of the boys approached and asked if we wanted our shoes shined. I laughed a bit and told him I was wearing sneakers; they couldn't be shined. But he promised he could clean them and make them white again. I told him to go for it. The boy next to him had a galvanized pail filled with ice and cold drinks, so I bought one for myself and one for the three of them.

Despite his quiet presence, the third boy stood out from the other two. He held his hand against him in an odd way, and his expression betrayed the fact that he clearly wasn't feeling well. I asked for his name and inquired about his hand. He told me his name but didn't want to talk about anything else. His two companions explained that the boy was scared because a cut on his hand had become infected and he worried that others would think he was contagious.

After some coaxing—and a little bit of friendly aggression from my friend O. B. James, who had been a lifeguard and knew something about first aid—we convinced the boy that his hand wasn't contagious and we might be able to help. As O. B. began removing the bandage, he was shocked to see a deep gash that appeared to go all the way down to the boy's tendons. The hand was, in fact, very infected, and the boy was running a fever. I once cut my hand pretty badly with a hand chisel, but this cut was in a whole different league.

I didn't want to scare the boy, but I told him that if he didn't receive medical care he could potentially lose his hand. When asked if his parents knew about the injury, he told the story of how his father had abandoned the family. As the oldest child, this boy was responsible for helping his mother feed the family. He worked for a butcher to earn money for food and other household needs. It was at the butcher shop that he had sliced his hand with a large knife while carving meat. The butcher had been unsympathetic and fired the boy since he could no longer work. Now that he was jobless, the boy was on this trip with his two friends to try to work to raise money for his family.

When morning came, the bus arrived in Veracruz, Mexico, a city we had planned to visit for only a day. I learned from the boys that they planned to work the streets for a few days, shining shoes and selling cold drinks to the tourists, before returning home with any money they made. We convinced the boys to change their plans.

I took the injured boy to the hospital, where a doctor took a look at the hand and agreed it was infected and would need treatment and stitches right away. He also made it clear that someone would need to pay for the procedures before the hospital staff would help. O. B. and I told the doctor we would cover the bill and that I would be responsible for anything the boy needed by way of medicine or further medical help. The cost turned out to be rather reasonable, and the boy began medical treatment.

We decided it would be best for O. B. to continue traveling as planned. I would stay with the boys until the medical treatment was complete and then accompany them on their trip back home.

Within a few days, the treatment seemed to be working. The boy's hand was healing, and we were able to make the return trip. I'll never forget meeting the young boy's mother when we arrived at his home. She seemed so vulnerable. As I explained what had happened and gave her what money I could spare and still make it back to San Diego, this mother exclaimed through tears that this was a miracle—a gift from God!

Indeed, a miracle had occurred. But it was not just the boy and his family who were recipients of God's grace that week. In that moment, I had never felt closer to God. More so, I felt as if the Lord had guided me to this boy and used me in a very powerful way. I was on fire! My immediate desires were twofold: I wanted to dive into a life of service, and I wanted to, someday, be a father to a child such as the one I had just returned to his mother. The experience became a marker in my life, one I have looked back on many times throughout my life and my journey with faith.

I returned to San Diego filled with love for the work of God in the world, determined to dedicate myself to helping others. I spoke with some of my Jesuit friends about the possibility of making the priesthood a vocation and joining their order. They kind of laughed and said, "No kidding," like they already knew this was a path I would take.

On August 23, 1983, I entered the Jesuit Novitiate in California to become a Jesuit priest. Although the Jesuits are Catholic, they do things much differently from other Catholic religious orders and diocesan priests. For one, the process to become a priest is much longer and more intense as you are taught to embrace the centuries-old tenets of the Jesuits. One of the first requirements is a thirty-day, silent retreat based on *The Spiritual Exercises of St. Ignatius of Loyola*, the founder of the Jesuits. During the retreat, you may speak only to your spiritual director. Most days you are allowed a short period of time to confer with him as you study and pray.

The Spiritual Exercises turned out to be a great gift in my life. For thirty days I was able to contemplate what it means to be a follower of Jesus, and I learned how to encounter Him in prayer in a way that has deepened my love of Jesus and strengthened my faith in Him.

The Spiritual Exercises are arranged in four distinct parts called "weeks" because they roughly correspond to a week of prayer. Each week you contemplate different parts of Jesus' life and how they intersect with your own. The anticipated result is a more intimate relationship with Jesus. The First

Week focuses on feeling contrition, tears, and sorrow for your sins. The Second Week dwells on the life of Jesus up to Palm Sunday. The Third Week involves prayer and contemplation about the death of Jesus and all that He suffered. Finally, the Fourth Week centers on prayer and study regarding Jesus' Resurrection and Ascension.

I approached the Exercises with a resolve to offer myself up to Christ so that He could use me as He saw fit. I prayed for generosity and magnanimity. I was twenty-two years old and ready to march to whatever mission Jesus was going to send me on as a Jesuit.

Throughout the thirty days, I learned to pray with new fervor. I learned to read the Bible in a way that required all my senses so that I didn't just read the words but transported myself to the scene where Jesus was teaching or preaching. I learned to feel the warmth of the Son, the feel of the wind, the expressions on the faces of Jesus' disciples, as well as those that doubted or hated Jesus.

This new type of prayer and study took more time, but it gave me a much richer experience in prayer. I felt especially moved by the passage in Mark (Mark 10:17–21) where the rich young man runs up to Jesus and asks Him what he must do to gain everlasting life. Jesus tells him that he must keep the commandments, to which the young man replies that he's been doing just that since his youth. Jesus then looks at the man with love. The idea of Jesus looking upon the young man with love pierced my heart, telling me that the Lord of all would look at me with the same love.

What happens next in the passage is almost as significant.

Jesus tells the man that he must do one other thing: sell all he has and give to the poor. The young man is immediately brokenhearted and goes away. As I read this passage, it seemed to me that Jesus, too, must have been brokenhearted when this man He loved walked away from Him. I didn't want to break Jesus' heart in this way. I wanted to continue in that moment of love with my God.

The impression stayed with me throughout the thirty days. The Exercises are designed to help you commit to God through what is generally called the "First Principle and Foundation," which states that we are "created to praise, revere and serve God our Lord." Additionally, it calls for the follower to be indifferent to all other things, whether they be health or sickness, riches or poverty, honor or dishonor, a long or short life. There are many other important tenets of the Spiritual Exercises, but the two that remain very important in my life are the "Call of the King" and the "Meditation on the Two Standards." The first asks that followers be prompt and diligent in accomplishing the mission that Christ might set them on. The second asks that followers see the difference between the standard of Christ and the standard of the enemy of our soul, who preys on us with deceits and snares.

Some of my fellow retreat participants couldn't wait for the thirty days to end because they wanted to share with the rest of us what they had experienced. A few just wanted some mobility back in their lives. I, on the other hand, didn't want the experience to end. I could have easily gone another thirty days without speaking to anyone and instead have spent the days in prayer in this new way. Because the retreat was nestled in the hills around Santa Barbara, California, I spent many days hiking the mountains while praying in that beautiful setting. It was glorious!

But extending the retreat was not to be, for I was called not just to ponder and pray, but to act. And so I asked to continue my efforts toward the priesthood with the Jesuits. Almost immediately, I was placed in a job working with elderly shut-ins and the blind. Next I was sent to San Francisco to live in a large Jesuit community and work at Seaton Medical Center as a chaplain. After that experiment—the name given to such work experiences—I was sent to Mexico with the intention that I would come to understand actual poverty; though as a child, my family had never been wealthy.

The second year as a Jesuit, or Secondi, leads to taking vows of poverty, chastity, and obedience. The first vows of a Jesuit are not to be taken lightly. In fact, unlike the vows many Catholic orders require after this stage of training, these vows are permanent. Because of their significance, trainees during the Secondi are placed in more challenging apostolates, or experiments, to see if they are serious about continuing the life of a Jesuit.

For my Secondi, I was sent to live in Los Angeles at a small, Jesuit parish that ministered to the poor in East Los Angeles. The name of the parish was Dolores Mission, and, though quite small, it was well known in the city of Los Angeles as a mission heavily involved in effecting social justice. In fact, it was probably the most socially active Jesuit parish in the California Province of the Society of Jesuits. I loved my experience at Dolores Mission and felt I was serving the Lord.

I was helping the poor, as well as the middle class and wealthy who were attracted to the Ignatius ideal of contemplation in action. My now-not-so-new way of praying was bringing me ever closer to our Lord.

While living at Dolores Mission and participating in many of the events at the church and elementary school, my main job was to work in Refugee Services. Father Mike Kennedy, S.J., a Jesuit priest at La Placita Olvera parish, was my guide in this endeavor. The Catholic Church in America had made a strong commitment to helping Central American refugees escape the terrible civil wars in their countries and had asked the various religious orders to take up this mission; so we did.

I spent most days in the homeless area of downtown Los Angeles around St. Vincent de Paul Cathedral, assisting mostly women and children whose loved ones had been murdered by death squads in their countries. I would arrange transportation to and help from different Catholic and Protestant churches willing to assist. I met hundreds of refugees during this time. I learned how to distinguish Salvadorians from Guatemalans—at least most of the time—and would sometimes even come across a family from Nicaragua.

I loved my job because it entailed working in an area I felt was unambiguously positive. The Christian churches had made a decision to work with the refugees from Central America, who almost all were Christians themselves, and I was answering that call and loving the Lord for the opportunity to work on His behalf. Little did I know the surprise the Lord was about to present me with.

I was at the Dolores Mission in my small cell, as they were

called, when I heard some banging hard against the door. I was the only one in the mission that night, so I went to the door where I saw a very short man who looked like so many of the refugees I worked with all day long. The only difference being that he was better dressed and his distress seemed particularly acute.

He begged me to hold him tight because he wanted to hurt himself. I felt a little awkward reaching out to him but, when his knees buckled and he fell to the ground, I helped him up and gave him a big bear hug. I can still remember how petite he felt (he was barely five feet tall, and I am more than six feet tall) and how his body convulsed as I held him. I asked him if I could call for medical help. He didn't respond to me in any way that I could understand; he just kept crying and convulsing. A quick assessment told me it wasn't medical care he needed, but God's care.

After a long time, he finally calmed down and I told him I was going to let go of him and that I didn't want him to do anything crazy. When he finally settled down enough to talk I told him that we should begin with prayer and ask for God's guidance. I always found that this calmed people down, especially Catholics, and it established that I was there as a Jesuit representing the Catholic Church. I also found it personally beneficial to ask the Lord to be present in the conversation. After we prayed he began by telling me that both he and his family were Catholic and had attended Dolores Mission some years before when they lived in the neighborhood.

Although it was still hard to hear fully what he was saying, I gathered that he belonged to a neighboring Catholic parish and he was adamant that he and his wife were married in the Catholic Church. Other facts started coming into focus, including that he and his wife had one daughter and that she had been ill. Then he tried very hard to tell me that he tried everything he could to help his daughter, even though they were very poor. He really wanted me to know how much he loved his little angel that God had given him and that there wasn't anything he wouldn't do to change places with her. I started to realize that his daughter had died and that he was in great distress over her death.

I remember tearing up myself as he explained how the doctors told him that his daughter had cancer and that it was going to take a lot of work to save her. He explained that he would take his daughter on the bus to the hospital and that all her beautiful hair fell out. He also said that he watched as she seemed to get smaller and smaller. He said that she started to lose the ability to do anything but smile, and then he explained how two days earlier he and his wife had gotten into bed with their daughter and held her hand as she breathed her last breath. She died, and the county came and coldly put her in a plastic bag and took her away.

He continually repeated his desire to change places with her in an instant if God would let him. He told me how he had begged and pleaded with the Lord to make her well. Eventually, he told me that the reason he had come to Dolores Mission and not his own parish was because we were Jesuits and, because of our reputation as Marines of the Church, he thought we were somehow more in touch and would know what to do. I, of course, tried to comfort him and assured him that his daughter was with God now and that the Kingdom of God was especially made for people like his daughter.

The rest of the night is somewhat of a blur, but I remember asking about his wife's well-being and going with him to the chapel to pray for his daughter's soul. I finally drove him home in the parish van and talked to his wife about making funeral and burial arrangements with their priest.

I had spent months hearing about and seeing death all around me. So many mothers I had worked with had had their children and husbands killed. I had become accustomed to their stories of war, military death squads, and grief. I knew that their loved ones' deaths were caused by evil men. Somehow, these deaths were almost explainable. There was a civil war going on and both sides were committing terrible atrocities. But a commandment had been violated—thou shalt not kill. These killings were not what God wanted; and I felt somewhat privileged—called even—to be working to heal the wounds of sin.

But this young girl's death was so different. Here there was no death squad. There was no soldier murdering under orders from a superior. There was no clash of hardened ideologies. There was no sin pressing in on her. In fact, in that moment with this broken man, *God* seemed to be the culprit, not evil.

I knew that cancer had killed her; and, of course, there really wasn't anyone to blame. But I suddenly wondered for the first time how my sweet Lord could have allowed this girl to die. I was devastated that God not only hadn't intervened to save her, but that He may have had a hand in the illness. I didn't have a moment of doubt in God. I knew He had heard this man's prayers; I knew He had listened but not intervened. I actually wished I could doubt because it would have been easier to understand that there is no God than it was to know that He doesn't always intervene, even when sought out by good, faithful individuals. But I couldn't doubt. Instead, I was heartbroken and began a new faith journey to understand why God doesn't always answer our prayers the way we ask.

As I had done frequently during my long retreat the previous year, I tried to place myself in the presence of Jesus and ask Him why. To begin with, I was truly mortified. In time, however, peace settled over me as I recognized that God hadn't taken this girl's life. In fact, when Jesus suffered the Agony in the Garden and was then crucified, He literally felt this girl's pain and suffering, as well as the pain experienced by her parents and, indeed, the pains, sorrows, and sins of all mankind. As I immersed myself in this scene, I received a great consolation that I continue to carry with me today.

For two more years, I benefitted greatly from my time in the Jesuits. The retreat, my work with refugees, the moment I realized just how all-encompassing Jesus' Agony in the Garden was: these all combined to strengthen and solidify my faith. At the end of four years, I felt compelled to let God take the reins again and point me a new direction in my life. I petitioned Rome to release me from my vows, which they did.

Three years later, I was married. I went to law school and practiced law in San Diego, my hometown, for a short period of time until I got the urge again to do more for society, especially for the poor. I ran for office in San Diego and was elected to the San Diego City Council and then the California State

Assembly and then the California State Senate and now the United States House of Representatives.

I learned in the Jesuits that very few experiences in life are unambiguously positive. My career as a politician has not been stellar or meteoric. I lost three elections, and I'm not a very good speaker; but through it all I've tried to keep my prayer life alive and vibrant and bring healing where I can.

I'm a Democrat and proud of it; but I try hard to work with my friends the Republicans where I can. In three years' time, I've discovered that it's possible to develop very close relationships with people whose policies I not only don't like but vote against routinely. I don't see them as the enemy. Quite the contrary—I see them and interact with them like the friends they are. I'm sure I'm like any other person, and I'm hurt when people I love and see as the strangers among us—the least among us that Jesus talks about in Matthew 25—are spoken about on the floor of the Congress as somewhat less than the brothers and the sisters that they are to us. But I also know my friends on the other side of the aisle think that my positions are sometimes less than what the scriptures command. Through it all, I try to see the hand of God. I'm not always sure how He's working in some instances, but I'm confident in the final outcome. I have faith in Jesus Christ, and in a world that He has already redeemed.

Congressman Juan Vargas was elected to the California State Assembly in 2000 and was appointed Assistant Majority Leader. In 2006, he served as Vice President of External Affairs for Safeco Insurance and Vice President of Corporate Legal for Liberty Mutual

Group. In 2010, he was elected to represent the 40th California State Senate District

As a State Senator, Juan was Chairman of the Banking and Financial Institutions Committee and served on several committees. He was first elected to the United States Congress in 2012.

Currently serving his second term in Congress representing California's 51st Congressional District, Juan sits on the Committee on Financial Services, including the Subcommittee on Financial Institutions and Consumer Credit and the Subcommittee on Oversight and Investigations; and the Committee on House Administration.

Congressman

TOM GRAVES

REPUBLICAN—GEORGIA

FOURTEENTH DISTRICT (2013 TO PRESENT)

NINTH DISTRICT (2010 TO 2013)

★

Religious affiliation: Baptist

Birthdate and place: February 3, 1970; St. Petersburg, Florida

Spouse: Julie Howard Graves

Children: Three children, Janey, JoAnn, and John

Education: University of Georgia, Bachelor of Business Administration in Finance, 1993

"IF MY PEOPLE, WHICH ARE CALLED BY MY NAME, SHALL HUMBLE THEMSELVES, AND PRAY, AND SEEK MY FACE, AND TURN FROM THEIR WICKED WAYS; THEN WILL I HEAR FROM HEAVEN, AND WILL FORGIVE THEIR SIN, AND WILL HEAL THEIR LAND."

—2 CHRONICLES 7:14, KJV

★

I grew up in very, very simple beginnings in the mountains of North Georgia. I did not grow up in wealth or politics. In fact, it was quite the opposite. I grew up in a single-wide trailer on a tar and gravel road. My parents were loving people. They could not give me a lot of material things. But I never knew what I was missing from a materialistic standpoint. I did know that I had parents who loved me and wanted the best for me. They taught me to dream big, work hard, and to achieve more than they had achieved. I was very fortunate to have had a great upbringing with my parents.

As a youngster, the one love of my life was football. It was the thing that really had meaning for me as a child and all through high school. In many ways, football was my life. I would wake up every day, thinking about the plays that would be called and how to defeat the other players on the football field. But the one thing that was missing, and I didn't know it at the time, was that I was not brought up in a church home, a Christian home. We never attended church. And, to my recollection, I do not recall ever being invited to church until I was sixteen or seventeen years old.

As a teenager, I had a friend who invited me to go to church with his family. I decided to go with them, and I ended up getting involved in the church a little bit. A few months later, there was a revival at the church. I didn't even know what a revival was at the time, but a young lady friend of mine whom I was dating at the time asked me to join her.

And so I went. The preacher was Jay Strack, an evangelist. I remember very clearly being at the church that night and realizing that, while I was a rough and tough football player and considered myself a jock, I had no hope, no plan, and really no purpose in life except playing football. That night, I knew I needed Christ. I prayed to receive Christ as my savior, and I made that commitment to Him.

It was a new beginning for me—a refreshing start. And I found that there was a purpose for me. There is a purpose for everyone, regardless of where you come from, what your background was, how "goody-goody" you were, or how bad you were. God has a purpose for you. I didn't know what my purpose was at the time, but I had a reassurance that God knew, and He had a plan for my life. I may have lived in an obscure, single-wide trailer in the mountains of North Georgia, but He knew me. So my life sort of developed from there. I ended up going to college. I was the first in my entire family to graduate from a university.

I didn't have many of the opportunities that others did because my family did not have the funds to send me to school, and I personally didn't have the funds to go. But I worked my way through and graduated from the University of Georgia with a degree in finance. From there, I moved to Marietta, Georgia, which is where I met my wife, Julie. We met at Roswell Street Baptist Church; I was in the singles department there with my roommate, and that's where Julie and I met for the first time.

My wife's story is the opposite of mine. She grew up in a church home, part of a stalwart family that called Roswell Street Baptist Church their own. She and her parents attended regularly. Her mom and dad were very committed to their church and their faith and still are today. It is neat to have that balance as parents now, with one parent having had no foundation nor example with which to work and the other who had a very strong foundation and strong example of a Godly household. She and I are a great team. We have been married for twenty years now and have three beautiful children, two girls and a boy.

Our involvement in politics was minimal in the beginning. We were not involved in political life, except through voting. But that all changed in 2001. Our pastor announced that an abortion clinic was going to move into our community. My wife, Julie, became founder and president of the local chapter of Right to Life. We used the spring and summer to hold petition drives and prayer walks in an effort to prevent the clinic from opening. There was an outpouring of support from the community, and many churches joined in. Ultimately, the clinic did not open, and the facility went into foreclosure. Not one innocent life was lost at that place. Julie and I went to the courthouse sale of the property, and it felt like such an incredible victory for our community.

We realized, then and there, that we had to be engaged in the political process. The next year, I ran for state representative, and I ran in a district where a Republican had never been elected. I felt that I was called to run, and we prayed a lot about it. Though I felt I was being led to run, I was still a little apprehensive. But God got my attention through Julie, and we ran for office for the first time. We worked hard with a team of supporters, going door-to-door to share our thoughts for a better Georgia. The hard work paid off; we won the election. The next day, the newspaper ran an article that said I had made history. So that is how my political career got started.

Nearly seven years later, our congressman decided he was being called to do something different. When that happened, a lot of friends reached out to me and told me that I needed to consider running for Congress. I had never thought about it before or even considered it, and I really thought I was serving my last term as state representative. My season in the statehouse was coming to an end. I didn't realize that a new season was about to follow.

We began to pray about it—Julie, the kids, our extended family, and me. We felt that we needed to run the race. We weren't sure we would win, but we knew we should be engaged in the debate. And a lot of people, even today, wonder how on earth it happened—how I won an election in a district that did not favor me geographically. Only a portion of my county was in the Ninth Congressional District of Georgia, and more than 40 percent of the population lived anywhere from fifty to seventy miles away from me. We worked hard, with purpose, and ultimately, we did prevail.

The road, however, was anything but easy. We had four elections, all within ninety-one days, consisting of a special election, a primary election, and two run-offs. We faced a lot of opponents along the way, but we felt that we were being called to service—that God was calling us to just get involved. I will never claim that we were called to win because I did not know that. All I know is that I was trying to be obedient to God and to be engaged where we were supposed to be engaged.

And now, here I am, walking the halls of Congress. It is clearer now to me than ever that God has a purpose for everyone. If God can take me from the hills of North Georgia to Capitol Hill, anything is possible if you dream big, work hard, and have faith in the Lord. It's been a tough but incredibly worthwhile journey.

I attend Bible study in Washington, DC, whenever possible. There are a couple of groups in which I participate. One of the groups meets on the first day back, when we come back to DC, after votes in the evening. And on Thursday morning, there is also another one held by the Prayer Caucus that has great people in it.

There is one thing that I would like to say about the people in Washington. There are men and women here of strong faith who are good folks, who are definitely doing the right thing. I didn't know it would be that way. I have talked to other members who have said to me, "I did not know if I would win, but part of my prayer was that if I did win, that there would be godly men and women there to join in prayer."

Many of us have been drawn together. We are joined together through prayer, as kindred spirits, or by joining in Bible study. We pray for each other; we pray for the decisions that are being made; we pray for our nation; we pray for those in our military who are faced with challenges and dangers; we pray for those in need in our districts when we have devastating storms or other crises. To me, it is so encouraging to know that you can set politics aside, and at the end of the day, we have men and women who truly care about those whom they represent. As representatives, we are servants. We are to be a servant to those whom we represent. It is nice to have these relationships and times of intimate prayer.

Oftentimes people ask me how a Christian can get involved in politics, and I tell them that it is not just about running for office. There is a simpler and yet more important role; they should pray. 2 Chronicles 7:14 lays out the plan for Christians and believers. If we want to heal the land, it is all about humbling ourselves, praying, and turning from our wicked ways. It's not about the next election. The Bible does not say that. It is not about the next president or elected officials. It is about believers turning from our wicked ways and seeking God's grace, praying, and asking for His forgiveness. That is the lesson plan for healing our land today.

Congressman Tom Graves is known by his colleagues and constituents as being both humble and inspiring. Before being elected to Congress in June 2010, Tom served more than seven years in the Georgia General Assembly, where he authored legislation to help small businesses lower the unemployment status of Georgia. He currently serves on the House Committee on Appropriations, and three Appropriations subcommittees: Agriculture; Commerce, Justice and Science; and Financial Services.

His many awards include being named United States House Republican Conference Freshman of the Year in 2011. He and his wife, Julie, are the parents of three children and active in their Ranger, Georgia, community.

Congressman

DAN LIPINSKI

DEMOCRAT–ILLINOIS

THIRD DISTRICT (2005 TO PRESENT)

★

Religious affiliation: Catholic

Birthdate and place: July 15, 1966; Chicago, Illinois

Spouse: Judy Lipinski

Education: Northwestern University, Bachelor of Science in Mechanical Engineering, 1988; Stanford University, Master of Science in Engineering–Economic Systems, 1989; Duke University, Ph.D. in Political Science, 1998

"THROUGH WISDOM IS AN HOUSE BUILDED; AND BY UNDERSTANDING IT IS ESTABLISHED: AND BY KNOWLEDGE SHALL THE CHAMBERS BE FILLED WITH ALL PRECIOUS AND PLEASANT RICHES. A WISE MAN IS STRONG; YEA, A MAN OF KNOWLEDGE INCREASETH STRENGTH."

—PROVERBS 24:3–5, KJV

★

I am a cradle Catholic, so I have been a Christian all my life. The area I grew up in was heavily Catholic and I attended St. Symphorosa Grammar School and St. Ignatius College Prep. Being a Catholic Christian has always helped guide what I do and has shaped my career choices. I was taught, especially in high school, that service to others must be a very important part of my life.

I've always been interested in government, politics, and public policy. My father served in Congress for twenty-two years before I did. He was first elected to Congress when I was sixteen, but he was first elected to public office when I was eight. Separate from what my father was doing, at an early age I was interested in public policy and fighting for what I thought was right.

When I was around eleven or twelve years old, I had read that fishermen in Japan who fished for tuna also accidentally caught dolphins in their nets. They killed the dolphins and dumped them back in the sea because they didn't want the dolphins and it was too much of a hassle to do anything else with them.

My friend John and I thought that something needed to be done, so we created and circulated petitions to send to the Japanese government asking them to stop their fishermen from continuing this practice. You could say that we were part of a much larger effort that helped lead to the "dolphin safe" labels you see on some cans of tuna today. That was my first experience working on policy and trying to have an impact.

I like to believe that everything I do is impacted by my faith; it is an incredibly important part of my life and in some ways needs to be a bigger part of my life; but all believers struggle with that. I'm someone who regularly prays; I pray before meals and at other times during the day. I go to Mass every Sunday; it's something I never miss. Faith is very infused in my life. Of course, there have been times in my life when I wished my faith were stronger; there is always an ebb and flow. And sharing my faith has always made it stronger. When I married Judy in 2003, for example, my awareness and focus on my faith increased significantly because our Catholic faith is important to both of us.

When my father was retiring from Congress I had a good opportunity to run for his seat. It was a big decision for me. Going into politics was something I had thought about early on in my life. When I was in high school I thought, "I'm going to go to college, I'm going to go to law school, and then I'm going into politics." That was my plan.

But somewhere in college I lost interest in getting directly involved in politics. I still had an interest in policy and politics so I wound up getting my Ph.D. in Political Science to enable me to have a career teaching it. When my father told me he was retiring I had just gotten married and I had never talked to my wife about running for office; it wasn't something I was thinking about. So I talked to my wife, and I prayed about it, and I asked, is this something that I should do?

In the end I felt it was the right thing for me to do. I was always taught at home, in church, and in school, that you should use the talents you have—the abilities that God has given you—to serve others. That comes from my Christian faith, my Catholic beliefs.

Certainly my pro-life views have been influenced by my faith. I believe life begins at conception, and that's something that originally came from what I was taught growing up as a Catholic. As I got older, I thought more about this. Now it's not just a belief that comes from faith; through reason and science, I came to the same understanding that life begins at conception and we need to protect that life.

There are not many pro-life Democrats in public office; there has been a shift, with fewer and fewer in the Democratic Party who are pro-life. People come up to me and say, "You know you can't be a Democrat if you're Catholic," and one of my responses is, "We need people to be out there evangelizing on the life issue. What does it accomplish to only spend time with people who agree with you?"

Catholic social teaching is also important to me, although I struggle with what that means in terms of the role of government. That is a big question that is debated within Catholic intellectual circles. It is a good debate to have because it's a complicated issue. At the same time, the view that government can play a positive and constructive role is part of what draws me to the Democratic Party.

I don't talk much about my background in academe, but I

do think it has helped me to look at questions from different perspectives and in a very analytical manner. When I was a professor, there was certainly a battle over the role of faith in academe. They are not mutually exclusive so it should not be a battle, but it becomes one.

Similarly, there is no reason whatsoever to say that you cannot bring a faith perspective into your work as a member of Congress. A Republican colleague of mine in Congress who was not happy with some of the actions of his party once suggested that a group of us should form the Faith and Reason Party.

My faith is a critical part of who I am, and why is that less acceptable than any other influence that people bring in? That's the argument I always try to make: Why is my viewpoint any less acceptable than anyone else's? Everyone comes with a worldview; mine is shaped by my faith, and hopefully my faith really is driving me. That should be accepted in the public square.

When it comes to Bible study and a prayer partner, my wife is the primary one. I speak with her every night over the phone when I am in Washington; I can't remember the last time I didn't. It is something that I wouldn't and couldn't live without. And we pray together. We are currently going through a daily Lenten prayer and meditation book; it involves reading and reflecting on a Gospel passage every night. When we are together on the weekends we do it at home; when I'm here in Washington we do it over the phone. She is absolutely critical to everything I do.

Here in Washington, it has been very valuable to have a

House Chaplain who is a priest and who is from Chicago. He is a friend of the priest who was pastor of my church up until a couple of years ago. He is someone I frequently go to. To have a chaplain priest from Chicago, someone who I can relate to very well, that has been invaluable to me. There is also a group of members who, once a month, have dinner with Fr. Byrne at St. Patrick Church.

The meaning of the First Amendment in regard to the "free exercise" of religion and the "establishment" of religion is continually being debated. I grew up going to Catholic schools and it was education intertwined with faith. Then I got my bachelor's, master's, and Ph.D. in schools without a real connection to any religion. So when I got my first full-time position teaching at Notre Dame I liked the fact that the Catholic identity was important there, although there was controversy about how it sometimes played out. I'm pleasantly surprised that in Congress we are still allowed to have as much public profession of faith as we have considering the way the Establishment Clause of the Constitution has sometimes been interpreted. But it upsets me when I see religion and faith being purposely pushed out of some places.

The question of how religion and faith fit in does depend on the issue; for example, we recently dealt with the DC school "Opportunity Scholarships." There are a lot of issues involved there, but one of them was, "Can you have public funds going indirectly to private faith-based schools?" I think it should be allowed.

One member of Congress I was close with when he was in the House was Bob Inglis, a Republican from South Carolina.

He comes from a very different part of the country than where I come from and a very different religious tradition. But I often accused him of having a lot of Catholic tendencies. He is someone who, because we were good friends, is very open and honest about his faith and trying to best live out his faith as a member of Congress. I don't think Catholics talk as openly about their faith as people from other faith traditions. When I was in grad school at Duke University, I had close friends who were Evangelical Christians, and it was the first time I had day-to-day experiences talking in-depth about religion and faith with non-Catholics. I learned a lot about how much we could teach each other.

When elected officials profess their faith publicly there are oftentimes questions about sincerity. Sometimes politicians play up their faith. For me, being Catholic, coming from a Catholic area, unless I am in a church or at a pro-life event, people generally aren't going to be comfortable if I talk about my faith. That's completely different from other places in the country. If someone from those areas came to my district and talked about their faith in a way that was natural to them, for the most part people just wouldn't understand. And you see those different perspectives clashing here in Congress. But hopefully everyone learns from one another, and we all come to have a greater understanding and appreciation of what it is that motivates us and drives us.

Prior to serving in the House of Representatives, Congressman Dan Lipinski taught Political Science at the University of Tennessee and at the University of Notre Dame. Lipinski has served on the staffs of the House Democratic Policy Committee and the House Administration Committee. Additionally, he worked for the United States Department of Labor and the Illinois General Assembly's Commission on Intergovernmental Cooperation.

Lipinski is the most senior member from Illinois on the Transportation & Infrastructure Committee, serving on three subcommittees: Aviation; Railroads, Pipelines, and Hazardous Materials; and Highways and Transit. He is also a member of the Science, Space, and Technology Subcommittee, where he serves as Ranking Member of the Research and Technology Subcommittee, as well as on the Energy Subcommittee.

He is well-known as a learned professional with a tremendous academic mind. He has a reputation as a problem solver who seeks to find a solution and then tirelessly works to bring it to fruition. He and his wife, Judy, live in Western Springs and are avid runners, participating in many races each year.

Former Congressman

THOMAS (TOM) OSBORNE

REPUBLICAN—NEBRASKA

THIRD DISTRICT (2001 TO 2006)

★

RELIGIOUS AFFILIATION: Methodist

BIRTHDATE AND PLACE: February 23, 1937; Hastings, Nebraska

SPOUSE: Nancy Osborne

CHILDREN: Three children, Mike, Ann, and Suzanne; four grandchildren, Will, Catey, Haley, and Christian

EDUCATION: Hastings College, Bachelor of Arts in History, 1959; University of Nebraska–Lincoln, Master of Arts in Educational Psychology, 1963, PhD in Educational Psychology, 1965

MILITARY SERVICE: Nebraska Army National Guard, 1960 to 1966

"WHOEVER WANTS TO SAVE THEIR LIFE WILL LOSE IT, BUT WHOEVER LOSES THEIR LIFE FOR ME WILL SAVE IT."

—LUKE 9:24, NIV

★

I was raised in a Christian home. My grandfather was a Presbyterian minister, so I had a good spiritual background. But my true commitment to Christianity really occurred between my sophomore and junior years in college at the age of nineteen, when I attended a Fellowship of Christian Athletes conference in Estes Park, Colorado.

It was at that conference that I first heard Christianity articulated in a way I could understand and relate to by people whom I respected. I can't trace the exact time or moment during the week that I made the commitment, but I do know the course of my life was set then, and I have never turned back.

Sometimes it is easier to see God's hand looking backward than looking at the present or the future. I believe the decision I made to enter the coaching profession rather than to have a life in college administration and teaching was a pivotal decision, and I believe that God had a hand in that decision, as I was able to impact more young people in a greater way through coaching than I might have otherwise in academia. I also sense God's hand in the decision to marry my wife, Nancy. She has made a great difference in my life, and we have a similar spiritual commitment and outlook.

My faith has enabled me to have a better perspective on

events in my life, and I have come to look at faithfulness to Him and His Word as being more important—the most important, actually—than results or outcomes. I lost an election for governor. It was painful, but I also sensed that it was not the end of the world and that I could make a contribution in other ways. As a coach, I lost important games that would have led to winning a national championship, but I also realized that the impact of a strong spiritual approach to coaching could be meaningful to our players whether we won or lost.

I attend a Bible study group here in Lincoln that meets every Friday morning. This particular group has been meeting for more than thirty years, so some of the members are getting a little older, but I have found this to be a meaningful time of fellowship and scripture study.

In Congress, I always tried to vote in accordance with my conscience and in accordance with what I thought God would have me do. I'm certainly not a perfect person, but I did feel that it was important not to cast a vote in a way that would be inconsistent with my faith. I would vote with my party if I felt that no particular principle or ideal was compromised. Otherwise, I tried to vote my conscience in politics and in the way I recruited and dealt with players.

When I was growing up I chose not to use alcohol, and this sometimes led to a certain amount of negative peer pressure and ostracism, but I do believe that eventually people respected my decisions. Putting faith in God seems to help one gain respect. It is my hope that, through it all, I have been God's servant.

Former Congressman Tom Osborne is still known simply as "Coach Osborne." He served as the head football coach at the University of Nebraska for twenty-five years and holds a career record of 255-49-3, thirteen conference championships, and three national championships. He served three terms in Congress before returning to the University of Nebraska as Athletic Director.

In his early days, Osborne was drafted into the National Football League by the San Francisco 49ers, for whom he played one season as a wide receiver. He went on to play two seasons for the Washington Redskins.

While in office, Tom was influential in the implementation of the Iraqi Women's Caucus, which greatly helped bring Iraq's first free elections to fruition. He co-sponsored the bill that governs steroid usage, as well as the Federal Youth Coordination Bill. He and his wife, Nancy, have three children.

Congressman

RANDY HULTGREN

REPUBLICAN—ILLINOIS

FOURTEENTH DISTRICT (2011 TO PRESENT)

—— ★ ——

RELIGIOUS AFFILIATION: Evangelical Christian

BIRTHDATE AND PLACE: March 1, 1966; Park Ridge, Illinois

SPOUSE: Christy Hultgren

CHILDREN: Four children, Karsten, Kylie, Kaden, and Kole

EDUCATION: Wheaton Academy, 1984; Bethel University, 1988; Chicago-Kent College of Law, Juris Doctorate, 1993

"For if thou altogether holdest thy peace at this time, then shall there enlargement and deliverance arise to the Jews from another place; but thou and thy father's house shall be destroyed: and who knoweth whether thou art come to the kingdom for such a time as this?"

—Esther 4:14, KJV

I had the privilege of being raised in a Christian home with wonderful Christian parents who had, in turn, been blessed with a Godly heritage. Because of this, I realized at a very young age (perhaps five or six years old) that I was a sinner, that I made mistakes and was far from perfect, and that I needed a Savior.

I remember clearly the day I prayed with my parents after Sunday services and again before going to bed to ask Jesus Christ to be my Savior and to forgive me of my sins. At that point, I didn't understand everything that I do now, of course, but I definitely knew in that moment that I was saved because of what Jesus had done for me.

Throughout my life, I have experienced different types of spiritual growth. There have been growth spurts, such as the recommitment retreats I attended as a teenager. And there have been times when I've felt things lagging a bit, especially when I've found myself unable to let go of materialistic things or feelings. I've learned that anything we can turn into an idol in this life—possessions, food, fortune, entertainment, and so on—must be kept in check. Our only focus should be the Lord Jesus Christ. The power of the Gospel to save, and of Jesus Christ's sacrifice for me, should be the greatest influence, on my daily life.

Recognizing what He has done for me and realizing there is nothing I can do to earn my salvation—it all was done for me—is extremely freeing. It takes away the burden of trying to be good enough or trying to achieve perfection on my own. Instead, I can accept Christ's gift, respond in gratitude, and share that with other people, wherever He places me. To have the privilege of serving in Congress, to be salt and light here, is an amazing opportunity.

I think back on the story of Esther and the challenges of the nation of Israel at that time, and Esther's uncle [Mordecai] saying that "for such a time as this" she had been called into this place. That is how I feel, and I have talked to many of my colleagues who felt similarly called to run for Congress for such a time as this. We want to be faithful every single day, not only in the votes we are involved in and the issues we are talking about, but also in the relationships we are building with our fellow colleagues, with our staff, and with our constituents.

I love the verses in Matthew 5 about being a light in the world. We are reflectors of *The* Light, Jesus Christ. We reflect Him almost like the moon reflects the sun. The moon appears brightest when it is in line with the sun—with few obstacles in between, and its face available to reflect the sun.

I am more convinced than ever that when I feel far from God, it is not because He has moved. It is because I have moved. I have put obstacles between us in our relationship; either my sins or other things that I am pursuing. I hope I can always recognize this happening and clear away the obstacles so that He can truly shine through me to my colleagues and my constituents, so I can be an agent of change, an agent of hope, and a preserver of what God has called us to be as a nation.

When I decided to run for Congress, I didn't have a master plan. It was something I hadn't really ever considered doing before. I really enjoyed what I was doing in my private career. I served as a part-time legislator in Illinois. That seemed like enough. But then I very clearly felt God calling me to run for Congress. I didn't know if I felt called to win, but I definitely felt called to run and leave the results up to God.

On election night, we didn't know what was going to happen, but we felt good about how everything had come together. But more important, I felt confident that we had been faithful in running and that whatever happened was going to bring glory and honor to God and glory and honor to Jesus Christ. It was a wonderful place to be on election night—to feel confidence that we had done what we felt like we were called to do.

Our success opened up a whole new chapter for me to share the Light. One of the things that has been particularly exciting for me as this book has been put together is to see so many other people who share a story similar to mine: they were busy doing something else and, for one reason or another, very distinctly felt the finger of God on their lives saying, "I want you to do this; I'm calling you to do this." It has been so refreshing to meet the number of believers here on Capitol Hill, to find politicians who are here not to advance themselves but to be faithful to their constituents and to be faithful to their Lord and Savior.

I was nervous when I first came up to the Hill. I wasn't sure if there would be opportunities for fellowship or accountability. I have been so pleased with the number of chances I have had to connect with other believers throughout each week.

On Monday evenings, right after first votes, the Prayer Caucus, which includes more than one hundred members of the House of Representatives, meets in a room just off the House floor to pray for God's wisdom and protection and healing in our land. We humble ourselves before Him, recognizing that the problems we face are too big for us and that we need His help. We need His hand, we need His guidance and His wisdom for us to be able to address the very serious problems of this nation and this world.

The next day, Tuesday morning, a freshman Bible study group gathers to pray together, to go through part of a scripture together, and to encourage each other. On Tuesday night I join a group of senators and representatives who meet to study the Word, and also to hold each other accountable. We have a dinner together and check in to see how we are doing in our marriages, with our families and our kids, and how we can pray for each other.

There is a group that meets on Wednesday as well, and Thursday morning is our prayer breakfast. Every Thursday before the prayer breakfast, a group of Democrats and Republicans meet for Bible study. Throughout the week, we have opportunities for coming together, learning together, praying together for one another, encouraging each other, and holding each other accountable. These are very challenging circumstances and very challenging times, but I am so grateful for what I see God doing here on the Hill.

One of my heroes growing up was my maternal grandfather, a Baptist pastor who had a great influence on me. Grandpa was a journal keeper. He would write down things that happened throughout the day—nothing fancy, but simple things he could do and did do to help others. He was a believer in the providential hand of God and felt there was always a reason for meeting and forming relationships with others. He wrote much about his relationships in his journal.

I haven't been nearly as good as he was at that, but during the campaign I was very faithful in journaling. It was a wonderful time to simply record what was happening. At the top of each page I would write "God sightings"—the things I saw each day that were miraculous, things that made me say there was no way an incident like that could have just happened.

As I look back through that journal, I see over and over again God's involvement in my life, His protection, and His gentle working out of circumstances that were beyond my control. Such reminders encourage and strengthen me.

One of my favorite Bible stories is the account of Joshua leading the nation of Israel across the Jordan River.

It was harvest season, and the water was at high tide, overflowing the banks. But God promised He would bless the Israelites as He had their ancestors who followed Moses into the wilderness. As promised, God stopped the water flowing upstream, and the people crossed on dry land. Then Joshua followed God's command to have a member of each tribe of Israel go back to pick up a stone from the middle of the Jordan River. He piled up those stones as a reminder to their children and grandchildren that God had protected them, had led them, and had stopped the water of the Jordan River so they could walk across on dry land. (See Joshua 3–4.)

I think of my journal as a tower of stones like the one Joshua constructed; it is a reminder of God's hand in my life, a testimony that He is good and that He has brought me to this place.

Congressman Randy Hultgren has served on four committees during his tenure in the House: the Committee on Agriculture, the Committee on Science, Space and Technology, the Committee on Transportation and Infrastructure, and the Committee on Financial Services. In addition, he has served on the Helsinki Commission, the Tom Lantos Human Rights Commission, and the Congressional-Executive Commission on China. He has formerly served on the DuPage County Board, in the Illinois House of Representatives, and in the Illinois Senate. He works consistently to improve prosperity, advance free enterprise, protect religious liberty, and defend the Constitution on behalf of his constituents and the country at large.

Randy married his college sweetheart, Christy, and they are the parents of four children.

Congressman

JIM LANGEVIN

DEMOCRAT—RHODE ISLAND

SECOND DISTRICT (2001 TO PRESENT)

—— ★ ——

Religious affiliation: Roman Catholic

Birthdate and place: April 22, 1964; Providence, Rhode Island

Education: Rhode Island College, Bachelor of Arts, 1990; Kennedy School of Government at Harvard University, Master of Arts in Public Administration, 1994

"IF YE HAVE FAITH AS A GRAIN OF MUSTARD SEED, YE SHALL SAY UNTO THIS MOUNTAIN, REMOVE HENCE TO YONDER PLACE; AND IT SHALL REMOVE; AND NOTHING SHALL BE IMPOSSIBLE UNTO YOU."

—MATTHEW 17:20, KJV

★

My faith has always been an essential part of my life. My parents instilled a sense of God and spirituality in my siblings and me. I grew up going to church on Sundays and went to Catholic school. But like many young people, I didn't spend much time thinking about this foundation of faith—not until it was shaken just before my sophomore year in high school.

For four years, I had served as a police cadet through the Boy Scout Explorer program. Over time, I came to love law enforcement and had grown determined to make it my career. My plan was to become a police officer and later an FBI agent. It was an exciting time. I had decided what direction I wanted my life to take, I knew what I was striving to achieve, and I thought I had things all figured out. On a summer afternoon in August 1980, however, my life changed in an instant.

It was the beginning of my shift at the police station, and I was in the locker room talking to another cadet, along with two officers who were standing nearby. One of them had purchased a new weapon, a .45 semiautomatic, and the other officer asked to look at it. The first officer handed it to his colleague. The clip had been removed from the handle, but unbeknownst to either of them, there was still a bullet in the chamber. The officer slid the action back, pointed the weapon into a locker and pulled the trigger. The gun went off, and the bullet ricocheted off a locker and sliced through my neck, severing my spinal cord. I was sixteen, and I've been paralyzed ever since.

It's been more than three decades, but I still remember those moments and their aftermath like they were yesterday. At first, the most difficult thing for me to comprehend was how severe the damage was. It wasn't just adjusting to the physical devastation and how it would impact even the simplest daily tasks and routines; I also had to accept the damage that had been done to my dreams, including the stark truth that my career in law enforcement had come to an end. I felt that everything I had worked towards and everything I had planned for had been ripped away. This is a terrible reality for anyone to have to confront, but for a teenager, it was almost unimaginable.

It was then that I needed my family, my friends, and my faith more than ever. The spiritual foundation that had always been there, but that I had never really thought much about, suddenly became a critical lifeline. After my accident, I drew on the strength of my faith more than I ever thought I would. It helped me through some of the darkest times in my life, and now I don't know how people get through challenges like that without it.

It took time. I struggled with plenty of doubts, questions, and sadness. But ultimately, I came to believe that God does have a plan for all of us. The old cliché that when one door closes, another opens—well, it has become the central truth of my life.

None of us gets through life without facing challenges, no matter who we are, where we come from, or what kind of opportunities we may have been given. I believe that those challenges are God's way of testing us, shaping us, and molding us. And we have a choice. When a challenge comes our way, we can curse our bad fortune, get angry, and feel sorry for ourselves, or we can embrace it, adapt to it, and grow from it.

I think faith is what helps us make that second choice, and I know it's what allowed me to move beyond my accident and accept a new course in my life. I faced a decision, as we all do. I could sit back and let life pass me by, or I could take what life had to offer and cut a new path.

When I think of my own experience, and what I learned from it, I am often reminded of a famous quote attributed to the brilliant sculptor Michelangelo. When an admirer marveled at a magnificent statue he was able to carve from a simple piece of stone, Michelangelo was said to have responded, "*Every block of stone has a statue inside it, and it is the task of the sculptor to discover it.*"

I believe that's what God helps us do through the tests, challenges, and obstacles we face in life. They really can make us stronger, and they can help us discover something beautiful within ourselves if we are able to learn from those experiences and move beyond them. But for people who don't have a strong foundation of faith to draw from, I imagine it can be very difficult to look at things from that perspective.

One reason my faith has been so important to me is that it allows me to accept there is a force out there greater than I am, that there's a path and a plan to my life. I believe that in many ways we are co-creators of our life experiences with God. The decisions we make, the life we choose—they are part of a partnership. We are never forced to confront anything that we aren't spiritually ready for, but through tests and challenges, we become better, stronger people. God opens the doors and provides the opportunities, but it is up to us to make the choices along the way that will determine the course of our lives.

I never would have consciously chosen to walk into that locker room had I known what awaited me. But spiritually, I now understand that it was part of God's plan for me. In closing one door, God has opened up others that I never knew existed. And my challenges have enabled me to experience and achieve things that I could not have imagined before my accident.

My faith has played an indispensable role in all of this. It has helped me to trust and to believe. It has allowed me to understand that I don't need to control every aspect of my life, but that sometimes it's okay to let go and simply follow the path that God has laid before me.

Along with faith, I've also discovered another fundamental truth in my life. When we face challenges, we rely on the support of those around us, and I believe that God sends the right people into our lives at the right time. In the words of an ancient Buddhist proverb, "When the student is ready, the teacher will appear." For some, that support comes from the family we are born into. For others, it's from the family we create. For most of us, it's a little of both. I certainly experienced that support system in my own life, when so many wonderful people—both loved ones and strangers—rallied around me in my time of greatest need. And that support is ultimately what inspired me to enter public service.

We all have certain gifts and talents that are unique. God's challenge to us is to find those talents, cultivate them, and use them to make a positive impact on the world around us. For me, that journey has led to Congress, where I can work every day to give back to all those who supported and inspired me when I thought an errant bullet had ended my dreams forever. With faith, perseverance, and a lot of encouragement along the way, I dreamed new dreams and found a new way to make a difference.

Congressman Jim Langevin began his political career in 1986 as a delegate to Rhode Island's Constitutional Convention and served as its secretary. In 1988 he was elected to serve as a State Representative in the Rhode Island general assembly. He was elected Rhode Island's Secretary of State in 1994.

Jim successfully ran for the United States House of Representatives in 2000 and continues to serve Rhode Island's Second District. His focus has been on national security, health care, and stem cell research. He serves as a senior member of the House Armed Services Committee as well as the Homeland Security Committee. He also co-founded the bipartisan Disability Caucus. He served for eight years on the Permanent Select Committee on Intelligence. Jim is the co-founder and co-chairman of the bipartisan Congressional Cybersecurity Caucus, and is co-chair of the bipartisan Congressional Career and Technical Education Caucus.

Former House Chaplain

DANIEL P. COUGHLIN

59TH CHAPLAIN OF THE UNITED STATES
HOUSE OF REPRESENTATIVES (2000 TO 2011)

★

RELIGIOUS AFFILIATION: Roman Catholic

BIRTHDATE AND PLACE: November 8, 1934; Chicago, Illinois

ORDINATION DATE: May 3, 1960

EDUCATION: St. Mary of the Lake Seminary, STL, 1960; Loyola University, MA, 1968; Honorary Doctorate, Lewis University, 2004

"If a kingdom be divided against itself, that kingdom cannot stand. And if a house be divided against itself, that house cannot stand."

—Mark 3:24–25, KJV

★

Trusting in Christ Risen's compassionate love, I would like to share with you some of my personal narrative as the first Catholic priest to serve as Chaplain of the United States House of Representatives. I submit this to you in the hope it will stimulate your own grounds for celebration of the truth that the Lord can use anything or anyone to shape the world we live in, to challenge God's people, and to invite people of faith to look more deeply into the roots of their religious traditions and draw from there the depth of their own being so they can bring their very best to create a better country and a better world by giving all praise, glory, and thanksgiving to the Almighty.

My life, my priestly ministry, and my prayer began to change during the ten days between my first interview for the position and the time I was invited to come to Washington, DC. I wondered what it would be like to be Chaplain of the United States House of Representatives. After ten days of silence and prayer, on March 23, 2000, I flew to Washington and was sworn in as the first Catholic priest to serve as Chaplain. I learned then and there when government has the will, there is a way to make things happen quickly.

I found myself in an honored position but in a whole new atmosphere of ministry, a secular place in need of healing, faith witness, and prayer. The need for a common sense of community and the challenge to find some prayerful moments for reflection were evident. It did not take much pastoral experience to see that the weight of the job of each Congressman was borne by his or her family. The one clearly articulated duty of the Chaplain was to begin each day of sessions in the House Chamber with formal prayer. My first prayer in Congress was stolen. It was an edited form of a prayer for the United States as a nation, written by Archbishop Carroll, first Catholic bishop of the United States.

About a week later, I was being led by staffers to visit the offices of leadership of both parties. Walking through Statuary Hall through a crowd of young tourists, I was stopped by a rather slight African-American who said, "You're the new Chaplain, aren't you."

I said, "Yes."

"Well what are you going to do about all the argument that was going on about the chaplaincy?"

"That was going on long before I arrived here."

"Right. What are you going to do about that fracas?"

I interrupted and said, "I wasn't here. I was in Chicago, a nobody—"

He jumped in and said, "That's it. You're a nobody, and you came here to tell anybody that there is Somebody who has grace and salvation for everybody!"

I was stunned as he kept moving on, becoming lost in the crowd. I swear he was an angel, because I remember each word just as he said it to this very day.

As I reflect on my eleven years serving as the Chaplain in

the United States House of Representatives, I recall that no two days were alike. There were no immediately evident patterns to an ordered life on the Hill.

Early on, my prayer, my words, my ministry were all being challenged to embrace the secular surroundings. I felt I was a missionary. I tried to stretch my understanding to embrace all the complexity and divisions within the House. I discovered the great diversity of assembled Congress members. I came to know them personally and appreciate how they worked to prove themselves to be true representatives of the very different people who elected them from a unique district back home. This truly was a huge country and very diverse. Yet "*e pluribus unum.*"

As a Catholic priest, in the past I had a morning routine which provided an easy transition from the priest's breviary to the missal of morning Mass using one good prayer book, then turning to another. But now, there was no public gathering of this community at my place for morning Mass. Instead I now stood alone with my own prayer. So each morning I rose to wrestle out yet another creative prayer, built upon revealed truths of faith that would speak to the real life of the members of Congress and the people of this nation. My desire was to unite them in a minute of reflective prayer, and using common language hopefully bring forth from them an honest "amen," but never to bring to the public opening prayer any political debate or an agenda item about to be brought up for a vote.

Early on, I was invited to the Abbey of Gethsemani in Nelson County, Kentucky, to join twenty other people, all of whom worked in government, from various parts of the world.

It was there I discovered and began to cultivate within myself some new skills I called "contemplative listening." This brought me back to Congress with a more careful reading of Pope Paul VI's statement on religious dialogue. I became a better listener to the scriptures as well as to the members of Congress.

I had shifted from a preacher and teacher to a listener. I spent more time in prayer, and I had discovered new ways of praying. I sensed there was a true ministry in just being fully present to others, focused on them, and not having an agenda for them.

When the 107th Congress began with a seeming solid economy in January 2001, all flowed in quite a steady course until September 11th.

On that horrendous day, a guest Chaplain took the prayer he had submitted for the record, turned it over, and wrote just three lines praying for a new day of peace and understanding. The gavel sounded. We evacuated the Capitol, with Congress having done nothing other than pray that morning.

As we wandered through the maze of national confusion, it became more and more a day of prayer as members held briefings every few hours, each one beginning with prayer. The police kept urging members to leave Capitol Hill, but they would not. They did not want the attackers to think they had been successful in creating chaos, causing Congress to run away. Instead, when leadership from both parties and both chambers decided to stand united on the West front steps of the Capitol, members insisted they would gather with them. After reassuring words from leadership, members themselves spontaneously broke into song: "God Bless America!"

That evening, filled with distress and questions just like the members and Americans across the country, I went to my apartment, anxious to talk to my family. I knew that the Opening Prayer for the next day would prove most significant. Trying to arrest emotions, I prayed silently. But when I stared at the blank sheet of paper before me, I could not write. So I turned to a faithful friend. I picked up Thomas Merton's *New Seeds of Contemplation.*

I jumped from title page to scattered reading of another chapter. "What Is Contemplation?," "Hell as Hatred," and "Faith." Finally I read on page 121, "If men really wanted peace they would sincerely ask God for it and He would give it to them. But why should He give the world a peace which it does not really desire? The peace the world pretends to desire is really no peace at all. . . . So instead of loving what you think is peace, love other men and love God above all. And instead of hating the people you think are warmakers, hate the appetites and the disorder in your own soul, which are the causes of war" (pp. 121–22).

With that, I threw the book to the other side of the room. I knew deep down someday I would have to return to this reading and deal with it, but at that moment it was no help. The violation of nation and world peace was too much. At that moment, I could not take it in.

I returned to the blank sheet of paper. It was in that emptiness of time and space that I recalled how the monks at Gethsemani begin their regular task of prayer. With the words,

"O God, come to my assistance. O Lord, make haste to help me"—taking these words to heart—true prayer began to flow upon the pages.

On the following morning there were more members present than usual as I prayed:

> *O God, come to our assistance. O Lord, make haste to help us.*
>
> *Yesterday we were stunned, angry and violated. Today, Lord, we stand strong and together. Yesterday changed our world. Today we are changed. We have humbly prayed to You, O Lord God of Heaven and Earth, yesterday and through the night. Now we turn to You for Your guidance and sense of eternal truths which built this nation as we begin a new day of building security and peace through justice. We mourn our dead and reach out with prayer and acts of compassion to all those families splattered with blood and exhausted by tears. Heal the wounded. Strengthen all civil servants, medical and religious leaders as they attempt to fill the gaping holes left in the fabric of our Nation. Send forth Your Holy Spirit, Lord, upon all the Members of Congress, the President, and all government leaders across this Nation. Free them of fear, any prejudice whatsoever, remove all doubt and confusion from their minds. With clear insight which comes from You and You alone, reveal all that is unholy, and renew the desire of your people to lives of deepening faith, unbounding commitment, and lasting freedom here where liberty has made her home. We place our trust in*

You now and forever. Amen. (Congressional Record—House, September 12, 2001)

Later that day, a young Congressman told me this story. After he arrived home on 9/11 everyone was relieved to see him. The family spent the evening watching the repetition of the terrorist attacks and listening to commentators. When it was time, he told his son who was four or five to get ready for bed. When he came to tuck him in, he asked his son if he had said his prayers.

The son responded, "Yes, Dad. But I did not know how to pray."

"What do you mean?" the Congressman asked.

"Dad, I wanted to tell God about those bad guys. But I did not know what to tell God to do with them."

The Congressman with tears in his eyes said to me, "Father, I was so proud of my little boy because of his concern not only for all those here in America but even some concern for 'those guys.'"

I asked, "What did you say to him?"

He told him, "You just tell God that you were really concerned about those men. Then trust God. He will know what is best to do."

From time to time, people may question the need for a chaplain in Congress or why secular government opens each day with prayer. But ever since 9/11, I have never doubted that the United States House and Senate will never do away with Chaplaincy in the military or the Capitol. True historic moments deserve authentic reflection and a call for transformation. Essentially religious people desire to be lifted up beyond tragedy and grief to a stabilizing transcendence. Religious leaders often serve ordinary people in a routine fashion. Extraordinary moments call for people to crowd together to lament, remember, and piece brokenness together as they seek healing and hope for a future day of promise. I look back on the nation's solemn prayer at the National Cathedral as a powerful example of America at prayer. It is regrettable that the momentary solidarity and heightened patriotism of 9/11 did not last. Perhaps it's because such moments seem so unnatural, people want to move on and struggle to forget. It is faith that leads to prayer and how to remember.

As the moral debate over pre-emptive war started, congressional funding for war was debated. Someone could almost measure the pressure to fund the war against the Homeland Security chart and whether it was yellow or orange or red. Those were terrible days of human energy, confusion, and arrogance as America tried to shrug off the cloak of humility and prove herself strong with new military technology, advocacy for spending money, television coverage of the invasion of Iraq, and a developing housing market. Perhaps that is why I found it difficult composing prayers each year to commemorate the annual anniversary of 9/11—until 2011.

No longer the official Chaplain, I was invited to Shanksville, Pennsylvania, to offer the Opening Prayer at the Memorial of United Flight 93. Ten years later, it was there that I found some closure. I was convinced, as were many others in Washington, that Flight 93 was headed for the Capitol—only eighteen minutes away when it crashed. Those thirty-three passengers and crew members aboard United Flight 93 departed from Newark to San Francisco on 9/11/01 and saved many lives on Capitol Hill. I think their heroic action performed under extreme pressure is a lasting sign to all Americans. As time goes on, I believe their example of courage and determination will become a hallmark call for young people everywhere: "Rip off the personal seat belts of comfortable security and join others in making a difference that can change the course a nation takes." On that September 11th my prayer was:

Here a prayer rises from hallowed ground
Made sacred by great heroic self-sacrifice, so others might live.
Here is found the beginning of a new national pledge of allegiance
Inspired by those who would grasp the few moments given them
to take matters into their own hands and make a difference. . . .
Ordinary people on their way to work or a family reunion,
offer on the altar of this plain
all they have and hold dear.
When threatened, they refuse to be paralyzed.
Finding within themselves an art beyond politics
they break the silence and decidedly act together.
They do only what is possible in an impossible situation.
Because they are Your children they find themselves truly free.

And so, this prayer offered at Shanksville on the tenth anniversary of 9/11 became for me a metaphor of the paralysis of Congress. The people on United Flight 93 were locked into their seats with seat belts. And yet they dug deep within themselves and found the ability to make an heroic choice. Once freed, they could act as one on behalf of their country.

Prayer for Congress, for the administration, or for the nation's courts of justice is always needed. But I believe prayer need not be born out of political perceptions nor lead to political criticism or public demonstrations. Religion should not be manipulated for political purposes. True worship calls for sacrifice—a handing over to the Lord. Praying with an agenda for others sounds like tax deductions . . . there are always strings attached.

These days I choose to pray as the child—I pray to the Almighty to be free of agendas, I name persons and issues but I trust God knows what is best. Assured by the Lord's relentless love for all, I believe, the Lord trusts us also.

Much will be left for us to figure out because the Lord believes we could be much better ourselves and work harder ourselves for peace and justice. Government often cannot do very much because as elected representatives they are too much like all the rest of us—and most of us are not ready to change that much.

Prior to being Chaplain, Fr. Daniel Coughlin served the Archdiocese of Chicago in the following capacities: Parish priest at St. Raymond in Mount Prospect and at Holy Name Cathedral; Pastor of St. Francis Xavier Parish; Vicar for Priests; Director of the Cardinal Stritch Retreat House; Professor as "Scholar in Residence" at North

American College, Vatican City State; and First Director of the Office for Divine Worship. While on a year's Sabbatical, Fr. Coughlin studied East/West religions, lived with the Trappist monks of Gethsemani Abbey in Kentucky, and served with the Missionaries of Charity in Calcutta, India.

Fr. Coughlin attended the University of St. Mary of the Lake/ Mundelein Seminary in Mundelein, Illinois, where he received the Licentiate Degree in Sacred Theology. He received an additional degree in Pastoral Studies from Loyola University, Chicago, Illinois, and an honorary doctorate degree from Lewis University, Romeoville, Illinois.

Now retired from Congress, he serves in the Archdiocese of Chicago and provides conferences on prayer and spirituality for various groups as well as personal mentoring and spiritual guidance for others.

Congresswoman

VIRGINIA FOXX

REPUBLICAN—NORTH CAROLINA

FIFTH DISTRICT (2005 TO PRESENT)

★

Religious affiliations: Catholic, Baptist

Birthdate and place: June 29, 1943; Manhattan, New York

Spouse: Thomas Foxx

Children: One child, Theresa; two grandchildren

Education: University of North Carolina at Chapel Hill, A.B., 1968; University of North Carolina at Chapel Hill, Master of Arts in College Teaching, 1972, and Doctorate of Education, 1985

"He staggered not at the promise of God through unbelief; but was strong in faith, giving glory to God."

—Romans 4:20, KJV

★

For many years, I have been encouraged by the very positive responses of people who hear my life story. My story demonstrates that one can become a success from extremely humble and impoverished beginnings, and my hope in sharing my story is to challenge others to work hard and trust God. Given my background, I am among the least likely to become a college president, state senator, or member of Congress.

My precept is that God has provided numerous opportunities throughout my life to be a role model, if I follow His lead and give Him the glory for the miracles He performs. There have been numerous mistakes in my life, and many more are made daily, but my constant prayers are for His wisdom and guidance to direct my life. God's love and support for David of old has always been a mystery to me because David was such a flawed person. While I am not comparing myself to David, God's love of David makes me realize that He can love and support others who are at least as flawed.

In my senior year of high school, an English student teacher advised me (while I was sweeping his classroom) to marry a college graduate and attend college myself.

This was my first consideration of college—no one in my family had completed high school, let alone considered college.

Financial aid was practically non-existent then, and funding from my family was out of the question; but ranking third in my class and having very good scores on the SAT made it possible to enroll as a day student at nearby Lees McRae College, commuting with three of my classmates, leaving home early and returning late to accommodate the varied class schedules.

After one semester, I dropped out to go to work in New York. I slept on the couch of my elderly grandparents' tiny apartment, working as a clerk typist near Wall Street. Six months later, I realized that New York was not for me, so I took my savings and moved back to North Carolina to enroll at Appalachian State Teachers College.

A friend helped me buy an old but serviceable car. I took a job near home waiting tables and commuted all summer until finding an extremely small but affordable apartment off campus. Because of my high SAT scores, I was exempted from freshman English and was even hired by the English department to grade freshmen papers. Again, life was consumed by work and school with almost no time for any social life, except for participating in the campus theatre, which I enjoyed very much. My plan was to become a high school English teacher. God had other plans.

During the summer of 1963, I met Tom Foxx. He was home from Chapel Hill, where he was a rising junior. We immediately hit it off and married after dating only a few weeks. In the spring of 1964, I moved to Chapel Hill, where our daughter, Theresa, was born in late May—a miracle, since I had been told it would be very difficult to become pregnant.

Tom decided, in the spring of 1968, that we should return

to Watauga, North Carolina, but the completion of my degree became a stumbling block. A visit with my advisor presented a real challenge. A change of major would necessitate an additional eighteen hours of summer school to earn my B.A. in English. A second opinion became vital when it was impossible to get all eighteen hours scheduled. A meeting with the dean of the College of Arts & Sciences resulted in a better interpretation of work I had already done. The remaining hours required was reduced to twelve, which could be scheduled—another miracle. Even in those days, I thought this was a "God moment," because only by the "Grace of God" could my problem have been solved.

With degree requirements completed, we returned to Watauga County with more miracles, as Tom acquired a job as assistant manager in the Appalachian State University cafeteria and I in the ASU library. With even more miracles, we easily sold our home in Chapel Hill and purchased a very small house in the Grandfather community (where Tom was raised) with a great view of Grandfather Mountain. Theresa was enrolled in day care at the Methodist church in town, and we were settled. Tom and I have always considered ourselves among the most fortunate of Americans to raise our family here. Life was good—God is good.

In April 1972, as my Master's degree was near completion, the Lord opened another door for me. A good friend contacted me to start a new program at Appalachian called Upward Bound, which serves high school students with college potential who come from poor families having no members who have attended college and little chance of their attending either. That was certainly my background, so I could readily identify with the students. The program had just been funded by the federal government and had to be up and running in late May/early June.

It was the perfect job for me. In the space of a year, I began two new programs at Appalachian serving seventy students in three counties and involving most departments on campus. I had no experience in the fields in which we were operating, but I went full steam ahead. The two programs became extremely successful during the four years I directed them. A large percentage of the students graduated and went on to successful careers.

I now fast forward to more miracles of God's directing the path for my life. On the Friday after the November 1984 election, around 10:00 p.m., I picked up the previous day's newspaper and saw buried in it an article about our new Governor Jim Martin's transition team. The article said that Grace Rohrer, a good friend, was on the team for the Department of Administration and was likely to be the new secretary of Administration.

After a brief discussion with Tom about a possible position in Raleigh, I called Grace and told her that I would be interested in helping her and Governor Martin. She invited me to send her my resume. Two weeks later, she offered me the job of Deputy Secretary of the Department of Administration and asked me to report as soon as possible. Appalachian was gracious enough to give me a two-year leave of absence. Again, I was the recipient of several "God moments": reading a day-old newspaper, Grace being a friend, ASU granting a two-year leave.

The job gave me an opportunity to meet many people in the political world that would not have been known to me otherwise. It also provided extensive experience in Raleigh dealing with both the legislature and the executive branch. This experience also later proved to be invaluable in my position as a North Carolina State Senator.

Just three months before I was scheduled to leave Raleigh to return to Appalachian, I was working on a project and needed to meet with the president of the North Carolina Community College System, former Governor Bob Scott. We had made several attempts to get on his schedule but had not been successful.

One afternoon, when I had some free time, I picked up the phone and called his secretary to see when I could get an appointment. She said, "Can you come now?" I could and I did.

In the course of my conversation with President Scott, Maryland Community College, in my home county of Avery, came up.

He said, "Did you know that the presidency of Maryland is open?"

I said, "No, but I would be interested."

The deadline was three days away. He picked up the phone, got me the proper papers, and wished me good luck. With God's help, I managed to submit a complete application on time. I have no question that it was God at work in my life again. Three and a half months later, I was named President of

Maryland Community College, only the third woman to be named a community college president in North Carolina.

In 1992 representatives of the Republican Party had called me and asked me to run for the North Carolina State Legislature, but I declined, knowing it was not the right time for me. I would have been happy to remain at Maryland for another ten years and then retired, but God had different plans. The party approached me again and asked me to run for the legislature, for county commissioner, for anything, but the preferred goal was the North Carolina Senate in a district no Republican had ever won.

Tom and I prayerfully wrestled with the decision, fielding calls until late in the evening almost every night. Finally, on the Saturday night before the filing deadline at noon on Monday, my prayers were answered and it became clear to me that running for the Senate was "the right thing to do." Theresa felt that we were taking a chance to get to the Courthouse at 11:45 that Monday to file, but I told her that if God wanted me to do it, we would be fine.

But getting the answer was only the first step. Now the real work began.

I survived a difficult primary, but we had no extra money for a campaign and were spending a lot for gas and meals to travel throughout thc district. Fortunately, appeals to friends made over the years resulted in our raising what we needed—just barely. In August, I came home one night around 11:00 p.m. after attending meetings and then going to grocery store parking lots to introduce myself to night shoppers (there are few other places that one can meet potential voters at that time of night) to respond to an important question from Tom. "Are you going to win?" he asked. "Yes," I said. "How do you know?" he retorted. "I just know" was my reply. We agreed that I would not be complacent but would work hard right up until Election Day, which I did, and we won.

Even if it had not been 1994, I feel certain that I would have won, because God was on my side. Twelve other new Republicans won Senate races to take the numbers from eleven to twenty-four in the North Carolina Senate, the highest number since the 1880s, and the House gained a Republican majority.

The Lord wasn't finished with me yet, however. Challenges were not finished, but neither was my time of service. In the 2001 redistricting, the Democrats put me into a district with another Republican, forcing a primary. Geographically, the district did not favor either me or my opponent; it did not even occur to me not to run. However, I wanted to avoid a primary, if possible. My colleague had been very coy about what he was going to do.

For about two years, legislators had had the privilege of attending a weekly Bible study on Wednesdays led by a wonderful teacher named Jim Young. On Wednesday of the last week before the deadline to file, during Bible study, an overwhelming feeling that I would win and that I should go to my opponent to let him know of my feelings came over me.

I called Tom that morning after Bible study to share my feelings and asked what he thought I should do about speaking to my opponent to urge him not to run. He said, "No, no. Don't do that. He won't think well of you in hearing that, so do not go tell him that." But later that day he called me back and said, "I've thought about it and think you should tell him. Maybe it will keep him from running, and you will not have to spend a lot of money running against him, and if you don't tell him and he runs, you will always wonder if it would have made a difference."

So I went to him early the next morning and told him, "Yesterday in Bible study I had a totally overwhelming feeling that I am going to win the primary and that I should tell you." He said he was still undecided but would let me know over the weekend (before Monday's filing deadline) if he was going to run or not. But he did not contact me during the weekend; I filed to run on Monday before returning to Raleigh and discovered upon arriving in Raleigh that he had filed to run also, putting us into the primary. We worked very hard, spent lots of money, and won with 67 percent of the vote to his 33 percent.

The election worked out, just like God impressed in my mind that it would. More challenges, of course, awaited. But so did more moments I knew were "God moments."

In 2002, we were still not very savvy with computers. We just did things the old-fashioned way: we got the list of primary voters, and Tom pulled out a phone book and wrote the numbers down on a list. I would sit in the bedroom during mid-day breaks and evenings making my calls. There were 1,450 calls to make in Wilkes County alone, and the night before the election at nine p.m., Tom walked into the bedroom and told me to stop making phone calls, because it was nine p.m. I told him that all but one person on the list had been called and I wanted to make the last call before stopping.

A man answered the telephone and I said to him, "This is Senator Virginia Foxx; I am running for re-election, and am calling to ask you for your vote and to answer any questions you might have that would help you make your decision to vote for me, in case you haven't already made up your mind to do so."

The man responded, "You just did."

I said, "Wait a minute, you didn't ask me any questions yet."

He said, "Well, I heard your ad on the radio a few days ago where you said that you were calling people in the district, asking their opinions on issues, talking to them, and giving them the opportunity to ask you questions. I turned to my friend (who was in the car with me) and said, 'I bet that woman never picked up the phone and made a call in her life.'"

With goose bumps on my arm, my response was, "Well, God directed me to call you, so that I could help you overcome your cynicism about people like me." That story has been one of my favorite stories to tell, because it is so clearly a "God story."

In April, 2003, Richard Burr announced that he was running for the United States Senate, after serving ten years in the United States House. The legislature was in session that day, so several people asked if I planned to run for his seat. My response was, "No," as I had never planned to run for Congress.

Later that night in my daily call to Tom, I told him what people were saying to me about the possibility of my running, and that they were encouraging me to run.

He said, "What did you tell them?"

My response was, "No—because I didn't think you'd want me to run."

He said, "On the contrary, I think you should run. You are in the minority now so it is very difficult to get things done. You'd be in the majority in Washington, and I think you should run."

So we talked a lot about it, started praying about it, and had a lot of people encouraging me throughout the next few weeks.

We finally decided that I should go ahead and take the plunge to run for the House. It became the most expensive Republican primary campaign in the United States in 2004. It also became a very, very nasty campaign.

In April of 2004, while working in my office I kept praying, "Lord, I believe that this is what you want me to do, but I don't understand why things are so negative and why it is so difficult for me to seem to get ahead in this process."

I decided that praying while working was not very effective, so I went down to my bedroom at 9:30 p.m., got on my knees beside my bed and began praying in earnest, saying, "Dear Lord, I truly want to do Your will. I believe this is what You want me to do. However, if I have misread Your direction, I would really be grateful for a sign. I feel too humble to ask You for a sign but promise not to be like Gideon and ask for more than one sign, but if You will honor me with a sign telling me if I am going in the right direction, it would be a big relief. I want to use my talents to do good, and I don't want my own ego to take me somewhere that You do not want me to go."

Before I'd *even* finished praying, the phone rang. It was Marshall Edwards, the pastor of Blowing Rock Baptist Church, where we had been attending. He said, "Virginia, this is Marshall, just calling to tell you that I am praying for you."

Well, I burst into tears, explained to Marshall what was happening as he called. I then asked him, "Marshall, should I consider this a sign?"

He said, "Well, I would if I were you."

"Marshall, please explain why this is so difficult. If God wants me to be doing this, then why are there so many hurdles in my path, why is it so hard?"

He thought a moment and said, "Virginia, it's not God who is throwing these blockades in your path. It is the Evil One who is trying to stop you." Well, that had never occurred to me, and it made all the sense in the world. He said, "The Evil One wants you to quit."

His comments changed my entire attitude about the race. That gave me the feeling that God wanted me to run, and I now knew that it was the Evil One trying to stop me. From that point on, my attitude was much more positive about everything. My high energy level returned and my burden was lifted from my shoulders.

Although I was personally re-energized, my opponents were able to out-spend me seven-to-one, as ours was a shoe-string campaign. We recognized the need for a poll, but we lacked the funds for one, so we drafted student volunteers who were already helping in the campaign. The results revealed that three of us were very close, but more importantly, we discovered areas of weakness that could be overcome. When the votes were counted, there was to be a second primary, yet another hurdle.

During the runoff, I happened to be alone at one point with my opponent. He said to me, "I cannot believe that you have withstood all that I have thrown against you. I expected you to fold long before now. Your stamina and your ability to withstand what I have thrown at you are amazing."

It was mighty bold of me to say so, I know, but he was rather taken aback when I told him that God had given me a job to do and that it seemed to me that he represented the Evil One trying to stop me from achieving that goal. Having the realization of what God wanted me to do strengthened me, and being obedient to that was not difficult.

About six weeks before the primary Tom and I were working extremely hard while being dramatically outspent, but were doing everything we knew to win.

One Saturday, we drove to the little town of Cooleemee in Davie County for a big community event. As we drove to the site, we passed the busiest corner in the community, and Tom commented that he would like to be able to place a sign at that corner for maximum exposure; however, we did not know the owner and put that on the list of many, many tasks yet to do. When we got to the fundraiser, there were about two hundred people in attendance sitting at picnic tables with only a few people sitting alone. We sat down with one of these individuals—a gentleman we did not know. In the course of the conversation, Tom mentioned that his task was to place signs and that he was interested in that corner site. The man informed us that he owned that site and would be happy to allow us to erect a sign. For Tom that was a sure sign that God was on our side.

Ultimately, after a hard fight, I won the runoff primary and the general election—another miracle from God.

Since being elected to Congress, the miracles have continued. They come so often that it is impossible to keep track of them. In most cases, though, I do my best to bear witness to them in order to glorify God. Sometimes, though, they are so special and personal that all I can do is fall to my knees to thank God. My hope is that He will continue to bless me with His grace.

Congressman

CHRIS STEWART

REPUBLICAN—UTAH

SECOND DISTRICT (2013 TO PRESENT)

★

Religious affiliation: The Church of Jesus Christ of Latter-day Saints

Birthdate and place: July 15, 1960; Logan, Utah

Spouse: Evie Stewart

Children: Six children, Sean, Dane, Lance, Kayla, Brice, and Megan

Education: Utah State University, Bachelor of Science in Economics, 1984

Military service: United States Air Force, 1984 to 1998

"The Spirit itself beareth witness with our spirit, that we are the children of God."

—Romans 8:16, KJV

★

I grew up in a family that reflected both the ideals of rural America and a much simpler time. My parents were part of the greatest generation, and they reflected those values in everything they did. I feel blessed that they passed those values on to me.

Growing up, my dad wanted nothing more than to be a farmer, figuring that would give him plenty of time to fish. But as the storms of World War II grew, he—like everyone else around him—put those desires aside and signed up for the ROTC flight program at Utah State University. He spent more than twenty years as an Air Force pilot before he finally went back to his beloved Cache Valley to farm. Meanwhile, my mother was a stay-at-home mom, which is no surprise when you consider the fact she was a mother of ten children. When I consider all of the gifts my parents gave me, my family is at the top of the list.

Not long after I was born, my dad decided it was time to teach his kids how to work. And what better way to do that than to finally go back home and buy a farm as he had been wanting to do for years. It turned out to be a perfect plan, for we certainly learned to work. I have always thought that any success I may achieve in life is because of the lessons I learned while waking up at five in the morning and going out to milk the cows with my dad.

My parents were fiercely patriotic, loyal to their family and their church and committed to protecting the freedoms that my dad had fought for during the war. After hearing them speak of these values for many years, one of my sisters cross-stitched a family motto and hung it on the wall: *This family's motto is Duty, Honor, Service to God, Family, and Country.*

This motto has guided our family for three generations now.

I grew up hauling hay, playing sports, and dreaming of becoming a pilot like my dad. Very much a small town USA upbringing. I even married my high-school sweetheart, a girl who is still the most wonderful woman I have ever met. Together, Evie and I have served in the Air Force, written a bunch of books, run a small business, and concentrated on raising our six kids. Life has been very good to us. We have much to be thankful for.

I think I have always believed in God and wanted to follow in His way. Now don't get me wrong, if you had known me as a teenager you might not have believed that. As Paul admitted to his companion Titus, sometimes I acted foolishly. But as I reflect on my life, I think there was always something inside me that wanted to believe. I wanted what my parents had taught me to be true. I wanted for there to be a plan. I hoped for grace and mercy and all of the things that make this life worth living. But for some of us—actually I suppose for all of us—faith doesn't come without paying a price, and life has a way of teaching us important lessons.

A few years ago, one of my adult sons was very sick. What started out as a medical uncertainty turned into something much more serious, and as the months went by, Evie and I began to fear we might actually lose him. He had dropped out of college and moved back home so that we could help take care of him. It was good to have him home but heartbreaking to see him suffer. Because of his illness, he could never sleep at night. All night long I could hear him walking through the empty house, pacing in the dark. Despite the fact that she had other responsibilities that required her attention during the day, Evie started staying up with him every night so he wouldn't have to be alone.

At one point, he had a doctor's appointment where they were to discuss the possibility of having a liver transplant, something that was looking like it might be necessary to save his life. My wife took him to the doctor while I stayed home to work. At least that was my intention. But the truth was, I didn't do any work at all. All I could think about was what was happening to my son. Why did he have to suffer? What were we going to do?

I was simply heartbroken. I couldn't think. I couldn't concentrate. The only thing I could do was pray. I poured out my heart, asking God to bless my son, to bless our family.

At that time God spoke to me in the same "still small voice" (1 Kings 19:12) that He used to speak to the prophet Elisha. The feeling was very clear.

Jesus Christ really was born. He walked the streets of Jerusalem. He is the Savior of the world. That's the only thing that matters. Everything else will be okay.

It's impossible to describe how this experience has impacted my life. It has given me faith and hope and encouragement in the deepest moments of doubt. I know the one thing that really matters. I know God will walk beside us in our trials, just as He walks beside us in our joys. I know that no matter what may happen to us or to the ones we love, if we keep our faith, everything that really matters will be okay.

I think that is true of our nation as well. And that belief has shaped my approach to serving in Congress.

When I was growing up, we always talked current affairs and politics around the dinner table. My parents wanted us to know it was important to be informed about the world in which we lived. Later on, as a military officer, I was even more aware of the special role the US played in bringing peace and stability to a dark and chaotic world. I also recognized the challenges we face in our domestic politics. But I never envisioned that I would run for office. I was an Air Force pilot, a writer, and a businessman. I loved rock climbing and skiing and spending time with my family. I was very active in my church, working in a number of positions that gave many opportunities to serve others. But as I watched what was happening to our county, I reached a point where I just couldn't stand watching any longer. I felt like I had to get in the fight. But I didn't know how.

In 2012, Utah was drawing up the boundaries for a new congressional district. One of my brothers called me one morning and said, "They have settled on the new map. You're in a district without a Republican incumbent. You should run for Congress."

And I knew almost instantly that I had to do that.

A few weeks after making this decision, Evie and I were talking as we were getting ready for church. We knew things were about to change for us and that these changes would impact our lives and the lives of our children. We knew it was going to be a sacrifice and that our lives would be disrupted. But we also realized it was an amazing opportunity to serve. Then Evie said something I will never forget: "Chris, remember, there's nothing you can accomplish in Congress that is worth losing your soul."

Less than a year later, I found myself standing on the floor of the House of Representatives while being sworn in to office and thinking of her words.

It's a great opportunity to serve in Congress. I tell my constituents all the time how honored I am to represent them. But I know some men who have gone to DC and come home lesser men. It is such a corrosive and prideful environment. And the only way to get through that is by leaning on God, leaning on the Spirit, and never losing sight of reason we are there, the things we hope to accomplish, the reason we wanted to serve.

And I'm not alone. Getting to know those I serve with, I have come to realize that many of them are good people. Many of them have sacrificed to be there. Many of them are deeply founded in wanting to seek and follow the will of God.

Often when we meet together, we start with the Pledge of Allegiance and a prayer. Many times we start with a scripture as well. After hearing some of these prayers I have often thought, "I wish the American people could have heard that prayer. If they could have heard that, they would have more faith in our future."

Yes, we have huge challenges ahead of us. We have to figure out how to get a few things right. But people ask me all the time if I still am hopeful for our country. My answer is always the same. Of course I am! I tell young people all the time, "You have so much to look forward to, such great lives ahead!" And it's true. The American people still care about their country. God still cares about this country. He knows we are the glue that holds this world together. And He still cares about this world.

Knowing that God still cares, despite the enormous challenges that lay before us, I am full of faith for our future.

Christ Stewart is an accomplished pilot, author, and businessman. A major in the United States Air Force, Stewart flew helicopter rescue missions and the B-1B bomber during a fourteen-year career. He holds three world records as a pilot, including the record for the fastest non-stop flight around the world.

Stewart has penned seventeen books and is a *New York Times* bestselling author. His books have been published in six different countries.

After leaving the Air Force, Stewart founded and served as CEO of the Shipley Group, a consulting firm specializing in energy and environmental issues. He resigned his post and sold the company to run for Congress in 2012. He and his wife, Evie, are the parents of six children.

CONCLUSION

Is America still great? Is America still good?

These questions echo in our hearts and in the hallowed halls of our nation's edifices of leadership. However, with the insight this book provides into the lives of today's leaders, hope is reborn that the answer is a resounding *Yes!*

Rarely do we see someone's true heart, but we are honored to have seen the true hearts of many of our leaders—hearts that belong to God and actions that are inspired by Him.

"God moments," as Virginia Foxx calls them, are seen time and again abounding in the lives of individual members of Congress. But Dr. Foxx has not attempted to create an exhaustive collection of testimonies of her faith-cherishing colleagues. This suggests that surely these are not the only public servants with a life of abiding faith. Many others' testimonies are not included but burn just as brightly.

It may have surprised readers to see how vital prayer is in the individual and collective lives of those serving in high office, and yet this book illuminates that fact as a shining truth. Weekly prayer breakfasts, regular Bible study groups, and conversations with others who also cherish God—these guide the relationships and inner lives of these men and women, and they strive to align their service with their values and belief systems.

Consider again just a few quotes from leaders in their own words.

Congressman Dan Lipinski: "I like to believe that everything I do is impacted by my faith."

Former Congressman Tom Osborne: "It is my hope that, through it all, I have been God's servant."

Congressman J. Randy Forbes: "Bible study is the most important part of my week here."

From these pages we've seen that leaders do rely on prayer. In fact, we've been able to see the very words of individual prayers, as in the case of Mrs. Foxx: "I want to use my talents to do good, and I don't want my own ego to take me somewhere that You do not want me to go." The humility in which they have sought office, often based on obedience rather than a personal desire to lead, is highlighted over and over again.

The connection they have to God also connects them to one another. As Congressman Frank Wolf said, "I was already a believer when I came to Congress; and my faith increased dramatically during my thirty-four years there. The bipartisan Bible study group that has met since 1982 had a particularly significant impact on me."

As Congressman Randy Hultgren said, "One of the things that has been particularly exciting for me as this book has been put together is to see so many other people who share a story similar to mine: they were busy doing something else and, for one reason or another, very distinctly felt the finger of God on their lives saying, 'I want you to do this; I'm calling you to do this.' It has been so refreshing to meet the number of believers here on Capitol Hill, to find politicians who are here not to advance themselves but to be faithful to their constituents and to be faithful to their Lord and Savior."

These are real people, with rich family and spiritual lives. Remember Congressman Fincher's words: "I love home, and I love the farm. I farm every weekend, and I still sing gospel music every weekend, and I give the children's sermon at my church every Sunday morning. I am just so thankful that He has allowed me to do the things He has enabled me to do and to make the journey while still keeping my roots."

These men and women are true believers. They feel a closeness to God and look for His guiding hand to lead them in their purpose. The life experience of Congressman Tom Graves taught him that "There is a purpose for everyone, regardless of where you come from, what your background was, how 'goody-goody' you were, or how bad you were. God has a purpose for you. I didn't know what my purpose was at the time, but I had a reassurance that God knew, and He had a plan for my life. I may have lived in an obscure, single-wide trailer in the mountains of North Georgia, but He knew me."

Mr. Graves also makes it clear that members of Congress lean on one another's faith. "Many of us have been drawn together. We are joined together through prayer, as kindred spirits, or by joining in Bible study. We pray for each other; we pray for the decisions that are being made; we pray for our nation; we pray for those in our military who are faced with challenges and dangers; we pray for those in need in our districts when we have devastating storms or other crises. To me, it is so encouraging to know that you can set politics aside, and at the end of the day, we have men and women who truly care about those whom they represent. As representatives, we are servants."

And so we read these things and we ask ourselves, "Is America still great? Is America still good?" The nation is only as good as those who live in its borders. If the United States is a representative republic, as designed by our inspired Founding Fathers, these leaders *represent* the citizens they serve. They reflect the lives and values of their constituents, the goodness, the faith, the importance of God in daily prayer and study of His Word.

When Congresswoman Virginia Foxx set out to create this compilation, she had in mind this goal: to inspire readers to believe that God still plays a role in the lives and hearts of those who serve in high office, and to inspire other men and women of faith to get involved and become an active force in local, regional, state, and national politics and issues.

Perhaps Congresswoman Sue Myrick said it best: "I look at my time in office as public service—not politics. It is another way to serve God. Heaven knows that today there is a big need for people to give of themselves in public service, but it is not easy. We get attacked by the press, and there will always be someone who disagrees with you. I would just encourage people who are of strong faith to get involved in public service, so that they can help change things. People of faith will always be needed to help lead this nation, particularly during the challenges that our country will continue to face in the future."

With the stepping forth of those who still cherish what the Founding Fathers believed in and who seek the hand of God in their daily lives, that goodness and greatness can live on today and far into the future for our children and grandchildren to enjoy.

The leaders of this nation—many, many of them—seek God's guidance in their lives, in their service. In the words of Former Congressman Steve Southerland: "I served in Congress with that hope, that understanding, and that expectation. But I was not alone. Many on the Hill are there in that same pursuit. I had wonderful examples to follow from legislators I worked with. Obviously there is evil, and there are people in Congress—as there are everywhere—who don't believe in these principles and want to pursue something that is more humanistic in form, and so you hear, 'Washington is broken,' and 'Washington as a community is an evil place.' I know of no place on the planet that does not have the ability to become an evil place. But I also know that God is there, in Washington—without question."

Indeed, God is still in our House.

ACKNOWLEDGMENTS

A book like this is certainly a team effort, and my thanks go to the many people who helped with this project, including my friends and colleagues in Congress who were willing to share their stories and their faith with me, especially Chris Stewart. Without his support and advice, this book would not have been published.

Special thanks also go to the Ensign Peak team who worked diligently behind-the-scenes to bring this book to fruition: David Brown, Chris Schoebinger, Lisa Mangum, Richard Erickson, and Rachael Ward. Jennifer Griffith also provided valuable editing advice.

Special thanks also to Lynn Worth.

And above all, I give thanks to God for His blessings in my life.

APPENDIX

The United States House of Representatives of the 114th Congress is comprised of 246 Republicans, 188 Democrats, and 1 vacant seat. About 98 percent of these congressional men and women cite a specific religious affiliation, according to the latest Pew Research Center report ("Faith on the Hill," 2015). Additionally, seven members are ordained ministers, and more than ninety members belong to the Prayer Caucus.

According to the Pew Research Center report, the religious makeup of the House is as follows:

Protestant: 251 members (57.7 percent) (Baptist, Methodist, and Episcopalian members top the list)
Catholic: 138 members (31.7 percent)
Jewish: 19 members (4.4 percent)
The Church of Jesus Christ of Latter-day Saints (Mormon): 9 members (2.1 percent)
Orthodox Christian: 5 members (1.1 percent)
Muslim: 2 members (0.5 percent)
Buddhist: 1 member (0.2 percent)
Hindu: 1 member (0.2 percent)
Unitarian Universalist: 1 member (0.2 percent)
Unaffiliated: 1 member (0.2 percent)
Did not respond: 7 members (1.6 percent)

BIBLIOGRAPHY

Barton, David. *Original Intent: The Courts, the Constitution, & Religion.* Aledo, Texas: WallBuilder Press, 1996.

The American Patriots Pocket Bible: NKJV. Richard G. Lee, ed. Nashville: Thomas Nelson, 2010.

Bacon, Donald C, Roger H. Davidson, Morton Keller, eds. *The Encyclopedia of the United States Congress. Vol. I.* New York: Simon & Shuster, 1995.

Brudnick, Ida A. *House and Senate Chaplains: An Overview.* Congressional Research Service. May 26, 2011.

Congressional House—Record

"Faith on the Hill: The Religious Composition of the 114th Congress." Pew Research Center, Washington, DC. January 5, 2015. http://www.pewforum.org/2015/01/05/faith-on-the-hill/2/. Last accessed February 20, 2016.

Johnson, Sam and Jan Winebrenner. *Captive Warriors: A Vietnam POW's Story.* College Station: Texas A & M University Press, 1992.

Manning, Jennifer E. (Information Research Specialist). *Membership of the 112th Congress: A Profile.* Washington, DC: Congressional Research Service, 2011.

Merton, Thomas. *New Seeds of Contemplation.* Abbey of Gethsemani, Inc. 1961.

Osborne, Tom. *Beyond the Final Score: There's More to Life Than the Game.* Ventura, California: Regal, 2009.

Price, Tom and L. Gerald Davis. *Saving the American Miracle: The Destruction and Restoration of American Values.* Charleston, South Carolina: CreateSpace, 2010.

Washington, George. *The Papers of George Washington.* Letter to John Hancock, 11 June 1783. http://gwpapers.virginia.edu/documents/george-washington-to-john-hancock-circular-11-june-1783/. Last accessed February 15, 2016.

Wolf, Frank R. *Prisoner of Conscience: One Man's Crusade for Global Human and Religious Rights.* Grand Rapids, Michigan: Zondervan, 2011.

ABOUT THE AUTHOR

Virginia Foxx and her family moved permanently to Avery County, North Carolina, in 1949 when she was six years old. Her mother spent her childhood in Avery but moved to New York (for work during World War II), where she met and married Virginia's father, a first generation Italian American. Western North Carolina and the high country mountains were an especially impoverished part of the state and nation at that time, and her family was among the poorest of the poor. However, there was a strong understanding of the importance of education and the need for an education if one wanted to advance economically and socially.

Dr. Foxx's parents, while having limited formal education, encouraged her to excel and placed high expectations on her. Fortunately, she loved to read, and due to very bad asthma and extremely poor eyesight, did not do well athletically, which allowed her to focus on academics. The influence of her high school teachers and principal prompted her to plan a career as a high school English teacher. However, having to work fulltime and go to school part-time prevented her from fulfilling student teacher requirements, so she earned an A.B. in English from UNC–Chapel Hill. She was later able to return to UNC–Chapel Hill and earn a Master of Arts in College Teaching, which allowed her to be able to teach at the college and university level.

The faculty at UNC–Greensboro allowed her to design her own doctoral program in Curriculum and Teaching in Higher Education, where she thought her professional career would always be. Her love of the written word and her inclination to teach whenever she can remains with her and eventually became the impetus for authorship in the academic realm.

Dr. Foxx enjoyed the publication process for *God Is in the House,* as it allowed her to use her gifts and talents to share with readers the heartfelt faith of our leaders in Congress. She hopes this book can provide encouragement and inspiration to Christians and future leaders of America in an analysis of God's leading role in our nation.